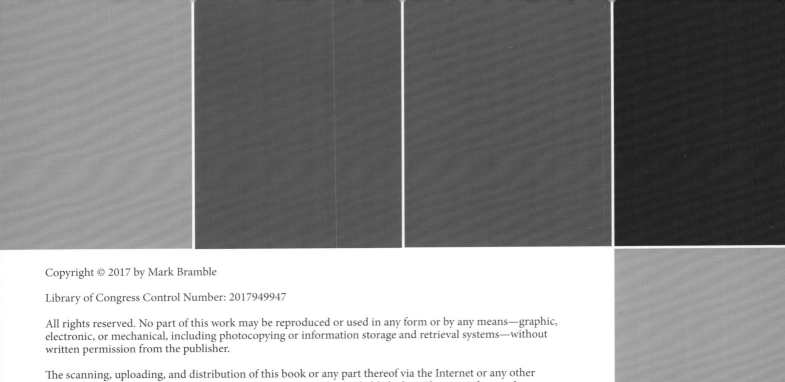

Designed by Justin Watkinson
Cover design by Justin Watkinson
Type set in Bodoni MT/Minion Pro/Optima LT Std

ISBN: 978-0-7643-5457-1
Printed in China

Published by Schiffer Publishing, Ltd.
4880 Lower Valley Road
Atglen, PA 19310
Phone: (610) 593-1777; Fax: (610) 593-2002
E-mail: Info@schifferbooks.com
Web: www.schifferbooks.com

For our complete selection of fine books on this and related subjects,
please visit our website at www.schifferbooks.com. You may also write for a free catalog.

Schiffer Publishing's titles are available at special discounts for bulk purchases for sales promotions or premiums. Special editions, including personalized covers, corporate imprints, and excerpts, can be created in large quantities for special needs. For more information, contact the publisher.

We are always looking for people to write books on new and related subjects.
If you have an idea for a book, please contact us at proposals@schifferbooks.com.

Contributions by:
Paul Vandekar, Deidre Healy,
Stiles Colwill, Graham Walpole,
Mark Goodger, and Margaret
Southwell. Photographs by
Benny Cuppini.

This book is dedicated to the memory of my mother

Margaret Kintner Bramble

(1918–2015)

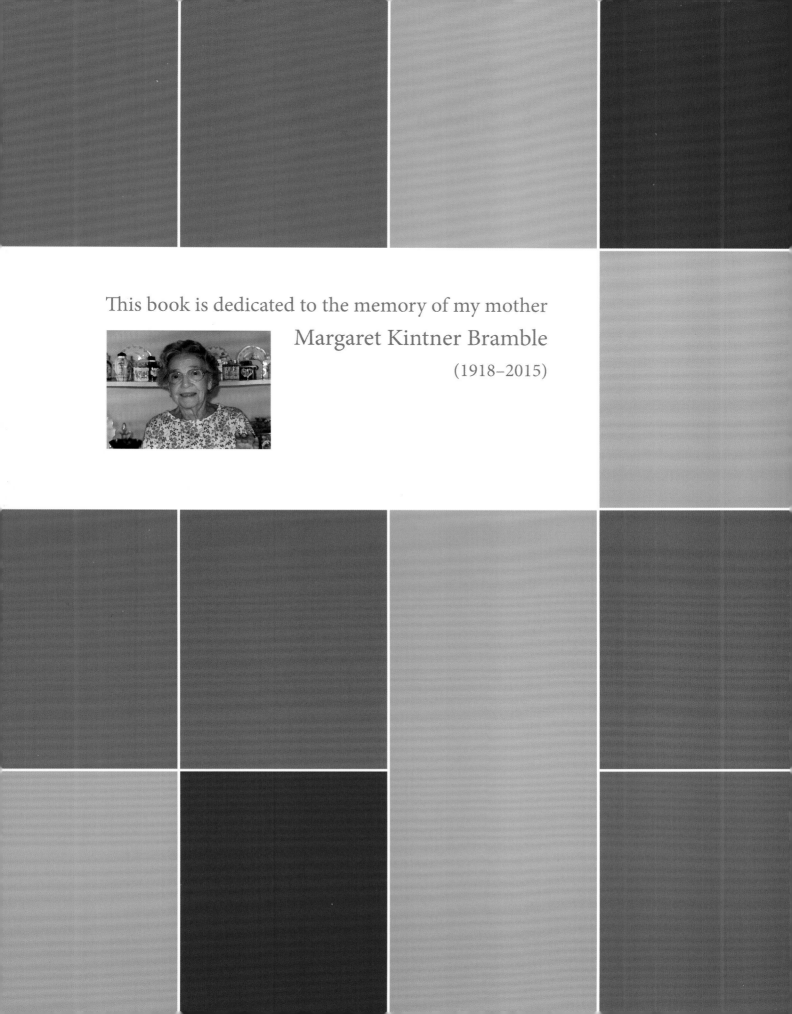

Contents

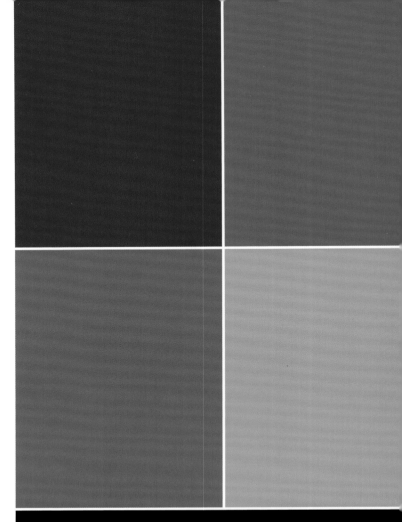

Prologue

Mother's first
tea caddy.

A selection of
tea caddies
from the
collection.

More than half a century ago, my mother Marnie Bramble began collecting tea caddies. She often said that as a petite person (five feet two inches), she was attracted to small things and was naturally drawn to the four-to-five inch, highly decorative containers used for storing tea. Mother said she acquired her first tea caddy in the late 1960s, without knowing what the little jar was; she was attracted to its "charming shape and size."

She soon learned that it was an eighteenth century Chinese export, sloped-shoulder tea caddy. Thus began her quest to collect and learn about tea caddies. She attended local auctions and estate sales in Delaware, up and down the Eastern Shore of Maryland, and wherever else in the world she traveled. Mother continued searching for tea caddies up until a few weeks before her passing in 2015, at age ninety-six. When I began traveling to put on productions of my Broadway musicals *Barnum* and *42nd Street*, mother enlisted me in her search for tea caddies. "Now Markie," —she always called me Markie— "let me show you what I'm looking for." We went to the cabinet where her collection was displayed and she gave me a tutorial. "These little jars were used to store tea at a time when tea was a very precious commodity. It was more valuable than gold. If you were wealthy enough to have tea, you stored it in decorative containers that would be brought to the table and the hostess would mix the tea with hot water in the presence of her guests." Thus began my own infatuation with mother's hobby. Over the years we have collected more than 400 tea caddies from the year 1700 through to the twenty-first century. This book is devoted to sharing our collection and what we have learned along the way.

Introduction

According to Chinese mythology, Emperor Shennong, known as the "Divine Harvester" or "God Farmer," is credited with inventing many agriculturally significant ideas we still use today, such as the plow, hoe, and axe, and innovative irrigation techniques. He is also believed to have made seminal contributions to the fields of acupuncture, the farmers' market, and herbal remedies. Legend also tells he discovered tea. As the story goes, while on a long walk Shennong stopped to rest under a tea tree and a servant began boiling water for him to drink, which was the custom of the time. The wind blew a few tea leaves into the boiling water. On drinking it, Shennong was filled with an overwhelming sense of well-being, and so tea drinking was born. As charming as this legend is, there is no evidence that Shennong ever existed and no evidence that he discovered tea. In 2016, Nature Publishing Group's open access journal *Scientific Reports* announced the discovery of the earliest known physical evidence of tea from the mausoleum of Emperor Jing of Han (188–141 BC), indicating that tea from the genus *Camellia* was drunk by Han Dynasty emperors more than two millennia ago. In his book *Tea Caddies Of the 18th and Early 19th Centuries*, Noel Riley explains the basics of tea:

> The tea plant is a variety of the camellia and its leaves go through various processes of drying, rolling and sometimes fermenting before being blended and packed for consumption. These methods have remained essentially the same for hundreds of years. When the tea leaves are fermented before being dried the resulting tea is known as black or bohea tea. Unfermented leaves make green, or hyson tea. Nowadays mostly we drink black tea, but in the 17th and 18th centuries green tea was nearly as popular, although more expensive.

The Chinese stored tea in ordinary containers made of ceramic material, clay, wood, or metal, which would also have been used to hold ginger, spices, chutney, and various liquids. There are no known examples of Chinese containers specifically designated for tea. In the catalog for the 2002 Stockbridge Antiques loan exhibition in London, Antonia Agnew, David Doxey, and Felicity Marno write:

Women Picking Tealeaves by Jun Wu Guangzhou, early nineteenth century. ©*Victoria and Albert Museum, London*

This paucity of 17th Century tea canisters in the records seems to be matched in the Chinese ceramic collections held both in museums and privately. For example, in ten collections of Chinese ceramics involving over 2,500 items and from different parts of the world, no tea canisters were included. The Garbisch, Veiga, and Hervouet collections between them contained only ten tea canisters, of which none were dated earlier than 1740. Even the superb collection of Chinese ceramics held in the Topkapi Saray Museum in Istanbul, which contains over 3,600 separate items, has only nine ceramic containers identified as tea canisters, of which the earliest are dated to the 1700–20 period.

In the early eighteenth century, we begin to find decorative tea caddies. We believe the word "caddy" comes from the Malay Chinese "kati," which means a measure of tea weighing about a pound and one-third. By the second half of the eighteenth century, myriad varieties of tea caddies were made. Of all the different items used in the tea service, the caddy is the object upon which craftsmen and artists lavished their greatest skills and materials. Today, tea is, after water, the most widely consumed beverage in the world. More than a trillion cups are drunk every year. It is consumed in almost every culture. In China, it is ubiquitous, from top executives in board meetings choosing teas as carefully as fine wines, to street sweepers and taxi drivers who carry glass jars with tea leaves and water. In Paris, it is fashionable to go to the chic Mariage Freres tearooms that have been in business since 1854. High tea is a daily event at The Carlyle in New York and at the historic Brown's Hotel in

London, where Queen Victoria used to take her afternoon tea. It is hard to imagine that nearly 250 years ago, tea was so rare and precious a commodity as to be the focus of the most significant event leading up to the Revolutionary War, the notorious Boston Tea Party. In 1773, tea was so valuable as to invoke the symbolic beginning of our separation from England, and our concepts of "taxation without representation." In early February 1773, the mistresses of three hundred families subscribed their names to a league, vowing not to use any more tea until the import clause in the Revenue Act was repealed. The December 1852 edition of *Harper's New Monthly* magazine printed the following pledge signed by women up and down the east coast:

> We, the daughters of those patriots who have, and do now appear for the public interest, and in that principally regard their posterity—as such, do with pleasure engage with them in denying ourselves the drinking of foreign tea, in hopes to frustrate a plan which tends to deprive a whole community of all that is valuable in life.

Instead of tea, the women drank "the balsamic hyperion," made from the dried leaves of the raspberry plant. This faux tea, and others like it, were known as "liberty teas." With the arrival of three shipments of British East India Company tea in Boston Harbor, the tea tax implemented by the Townshend Revenue Act 1767 had to be paid by December 17. Starting with the arrival of the first ship at the end of November, pamphlets circulated by the Sons Of Liberty appeared on Boston streets proclaiming: "Friends! Brethren! Countrymen! That worst of plagues, the detested tea shipped

for this port by the East India Company, is now arrived in the Harbor; the hour of destruction, or manly opposition to the machinations of tyranny stares you in the face . . . ." The night of December 16, 1773, the night before the taxes were due, the famous Boston Tea Party took place. In their book *The New Tea Companion*, Jane Pettigrew and Bruce Richardson write:

> To cries of "Boston harbor a teapot tonight" and "The Mohawks are coming," the three ships were boarded by a band of men disguised as Native Americans and for the following three hours 340 chests of tea were split open with hatchets and the tea hurled overboard into Boston harbor . . . However, tea did not disappear from American homes altogether. Direct trade with China was established in 1784, and George Washington . . . gave instructions during the War of Independence that all officers and men received a regular supply of tea.

Tea drinking was introduced to Europe in 1610, when the Dutch East India Company brought tea back to the Netherlands from Asia. Tea became extremely valuable, selling in Europe at extravagant prices. It is a delicate substance and great care was taken storing it. By the early eighteenth century, well-to-do households had lockable wooden tea chests holding canisters of the precious leaves. The chests would house two separate containers: one for black tea and one for green tea. This evolved into a three-container chest, with the third, center container made of glass. Some believe this glass container was used for mixing a blend of teas, but there is no evidence that it was mixed at the table. In his 1745 book *Directions To Servants*, Jonathan

Swift writes: "the invention of small chests and trunks, with lock and key, wherein they keep the tea and sugar, without which it is impossible for the waiting maid to live . . .", documenting that this center container was for sugar. These caddies were fitted with locks to protect the precious contents from thieves and light-fingered servants, with the key held by the lady of the house. The style and construction of these lockable boxes reflected the value of their contents; the standards of workmanship and design were commensurate with fine quality eighteenth- and early-nineteenth-century furniture. Caddies were made of wood, silver, pewter, tortoiseshell, mother-of-pearl, and ivory. The most unusual type of wooden caddies, and among the most desirable, are fruit forms. Apples and pears are the most common, but peaches, pineapples, melons, pumpkins, and aubergine also exist, often made in the fruit wood they depict. These caddies are made by hand-turning on a lathe, which differs from other forms of woodworking in that the wood is moving while a stationary tool is used to shape it. Fruit caddies have a single storage compartment lined with lead foil to protect the tea from moisture, and are fitted with locks and escutcheons of iron, silver, or steel. The finest of these were made in England in the late eighteenth century during the reign of George III, and in Germany at the beginning of the nineteenth century. Some of these are painted, but many have plain polished finishes. Although the Dutch introduced tea to the Netherlands, it is now well known that it was very popular in France, first arriving in Paris in 1636, two decades before it appeared in England. Tea was very popular with the aristocracy, and it is very likely this is where the concept of afternoon tea began. One of the first French tea connoisseurs was Louis XIV. In *The French Art Of Tea* Mariage Freres writes: "It is reported that in 1665 his doctors prescribed tea 'to aid digestion.' The King, having also been told that neither the Chinese nor Japanese suffered from gout or cardiac disorders, drank tea regularly for his health." Madame de Sévigné (1626–1696), in one of many gossipy letters to her daughter, wrote:

> I have seen the Princess de Taranto . . . every day she drinks fourteen or fifteen large dishes of tea. She prepares it as we do; first letting the leaves infuse, and then filling the cup half-full with boiling water: she says it has been the panacea of all her disorders; and she very gravely assured me, that the Landgrave, her nephew, drank forty dishes every morning. "Thirty, perhaps, madam," said I. "Oh no! I assure you he drank forty, and was raised by it from the grave.

Madame de Sévigné also reported that it was a French woman, the Marquise de la Sablière, who initiated the fashion of adding milk to tea, "from choice of taste." John J. Conley's *The Suspicion of Virtue* suggests more practical reasons: "Mme. de la Sabliere introduced a minor revolution in tea drinking. In order to preserve her eggshell teacups from over hot tea, she began the custom of pouring milk into tea." It is believed that Tomas Garway (or Garraway)

first served tea in his coffeehouse in London about 1658, but it did not become popular until several years later. In 1662, Princess Catherine of Braganza of Portugal married Charles II of Britain, who was living in exile in The Hague during the English Civil War. While in Holland Charles became a tea drinker, as was Catherine of Braganza, which was common among Portuguese nobility. They were instrumental in the popularization of tea in Britain. Soon tea mania swept the country, and it became the beverage of choice in English society. Poet and politician Edmund Waller (1606–1687) wrote the poem *Of Tea, Commended By Her Majesty*, to celebrate Queen Catherine's birthday:

> Venus her Myrtle, Phoebus has his bays;
> Tea both excels, which she vouchsafes to praise.
> The best of Queens, the best of herbs, we owe
> To that bold nation which the way did show
> To the fair region where the sun doth rise,
> Whose rich productions we so justly prize.
> The Muse's friend, tea does our fancy aid,
> Repress those vapors which the head invade,
> And keeps the palace of the soul serene,
> Fit on her birthday to salute the Queen

By 1700, tea was for sale in more than 500 coffeehouses in London. In 1706, Thomas Twining transformed a coffeehouse at 213 Strand into Twining's Tea House, which has been in business at that location ever since. Tea drinking became even more popular when Queen Anne (1665–1714) chose tea over ale as her regular breakfast drink. The magazine *Tatler* commented in 1710 that breakfast no longer consisted of "three rumps of beef," but that "tea and bread and butter . . . have of late prevailed." By the middle of the eighteenth century tea was a popular mealtime beverage. In her book *Tea Caddies: An Illustrated History*, published by the Victoria and Albert Museum, Gillian Walkling writes, "the provision of tea 'twice daily' had even become a condition of employment, particularly amongst domestic servants . . . by providing an alternative to gin it did at least help to relieve the serious problem of alcoholism which was rife amongst the urban working class." The official British import figures for 1750–1783 show an average of four million pounds of tea per year, all of it imported from China. It was not until 1838 that tea trade with India began. Ms. Walkling writes: "This was estimated even at the time to represent less than half annual domestic consumption. Smuggled tea was obviously consumed with little conscience as an entry in the diary of Parson Woodford in 1777 shows. 'Andrews the smuggler brought me this night about 11 o'clock a bag of Hyson Tea 6 pound weight. He frightened us a little by whistling under the Parlor window just as we were going to bed.'" In many European countries, the popularity of tea was eclipsed by a preference for coffee. Why? Taste. Tea was often bitter and required milk and expensive sugar to make it palatable, and if drunk on an empty stomach, the tannin in strong black tea can bring on nausea and even dry heaving. Coffee, on the other hand, was perfectly pleasant to drink without milk or sugar; it tasted

Masquerade at Mrs. Cornely's. ©Victoria and Albert Museum, London

better and cost less. Additionally, the trade routes for importing coffee were shorter than those for tea. Coffee could easily be brought in from North Africa and the Near East, but tea generally had to come from far away China by ship, and people simply did not think tea was worth the cost. The British could not get enough tea, and it became a national obsession and a catalyst for fascinating social change. In *Antique Boxes, Tea Caddies & Society*, Antigone Clarke and Joseph O'Kelly note:

> In public, tea was served where life could be witnessed at its most socially chaotic. In fact, tea was sometimes served in quite bizarre circumstances . . . Fannie Burney, the eighteenth century writer, diarist, and royal protégé records how . . . "We . . . drank tea at Lady Dalston's" which was quite proper. However . . . another lady who offered tea . . . was Mrs. Cornely . . . one of those larger than life personalities, who strode boldly through the social structure of the eighteenth century . . . Teresa Cornely moved to London in the middle of the century and set herself up in "Carlisle House" (and) . . . created in her London house caves and grottos as well as two Chinese tea rooms . . . Mrs. Cornelys offered many attractions and entertainments including singing and staging of operas! . . . In addition to the formal entertainment, a major excitement of such "salons" was the opportunity to rub shoulders with people outside one's own social stratosphere. The upper classes were fascinated by more worldly individuals. There was a frisson

in mingling with adventurers and even conceivably raffish characters. For their part, the opportunists liked the idea of elevated and potentially useful acquaintance . . . and for a few decades this peculiar business thrived . . . Even as late as 1865, Lewis Carroll led Alice's footsteps to the Mad Hatter's tea party, a social occasion perfectly suited to a fantastical world. Tea drinking was part of Cathay [an alternate word for China] and the dream of freedom from the social straightjacket. A person was allowed to drink it, even in dubious company . . . the tea caddy was the pivotal prop of the whole performance. After all, the precious leaf was kept safely locked in the curious little container.

The influential East India Company, founded by Queen Elizabeth I in 1600, controlled, among other things, the tea trade in Great Britain. By the mid-eighteenth century the company had fallen on hard times, partly because of bad management, but also because of smuggling. By 1784, custom and excise duties on tea were 119 percent, reinforcing its availability only to the wealthy. One pound of tea cost as much as a skilled worker's weekly wage. The value of tea made it worthy contraband, and the black market thrived enough to have a substantial impact on the coffers of the East India Company. William Pitt the Younger, Britain's prime minister and an astute businessman, knew that the most effective way to eliminate smuggling was to reduce prices enough to make the illicit trade unprofitable. The Commutation Act of 1784 reduced duties on tea from 119

Advertisement for the East India Tea Company. ©*Victoria and Albert Museum, London*

to 12.5 percent, resulting in a booming business across all classes which replenished the fortunes of the East India Company and secured tea as Britain's beverage of choice.

This flourishing tea frenzy provided a tremendous increase in the manufacturing and importing of tea wares, including tea caddies. Of all materials used for making tea caddies, porcelain was the most popular and has the most fascinating history. Venetian explorer Marco Polo visited Asia and China in the late thirteenth century. When he returned to Italy, one of his most compelling recollections was his description of seeing porcelain for the first time. He called it "porcellana" because of its resemblance to the translucent surface of the cowrie shell. The story of European porcelain has all the mystery, theatricality, and intrigue of grand opera. After the establishment of a Portuguese trading post on Macao in 1557, the first examples of Chinese porcelain found their way to the courts of Europe, where its glistening surface and translucency were instantly recognized as being much finer than any European pottery. Porcelain was greatly admired for its technical perfection, its hardness, light weight, and fine sound, all of which were very appealing. In the eighteenth century, porcelain was not just an art to amuse and delight the eye, but also a potent symbol of prestige and a demonstration of power. The French and English tried to make porcelain, but were unsuccessful until the 1760s, when they independently discovered the secrets of true porcelain. The first European porcelain was made in Germany in 1710. This is not

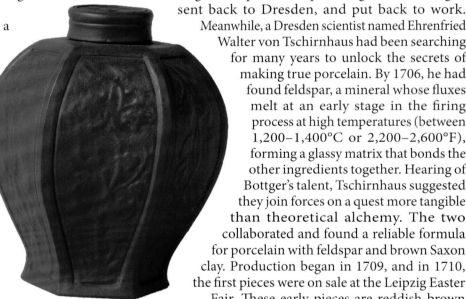

Meissen Böttger tea caddy and cover, c. 1715. *Courtesy of the Rijksmuseum, Amsterdam*

surprising, since the exuberant art-loving August The Strong (1670–1733) was the first famous German porcelain collector; his collection was unrivaled in Europe. He accumulated great debt as he financed wars, built palaces and museums, and added to his porcelain collection, and he was desperate to find some way to replenish his treasury. In his book *German And Austrian Porcelain* George W. Ware states: "many stories were told about his indulgence in acquiring porcelain. One related that he traded 12 'big men' from his personal guard to the King of Prussia for 48 beautiful porcelain vases which were jokingly referred to as 'soldier vases,' or in German, 'Dragonervasen.'" In 1700, Augustus learned about an eighteen-year-old pharmacist in Wittenberg named Johann Friedrich Bottger who was also rumored to be an alchemist. Hoping to make gold to replenish his coffers, Augustus had Bottger arrested, brought to Dresden, confined in a laboratory, and forced to carry on his futile experiments. In 1703, Bottger attempted to escape to Prague but was caught, sent back to Dresden, and put back to work. Meanwhile, a Dresden scientist named Ehrenfried Walter von Tschirnhaus had been searching for many years to unlock the secrets of making true porcelain. By 1706, he had found feldspar, a mineral whose fluxes melt at an early stage in the firing process at high temperatures (between 1,200–1,400°C or 2,200–2,600°F), forming a glassy matrix that bonds the other ingredients together. Hearing of Bottger's talent, Tschirnhaus suggested they join forces on a quest more tangible than theoretical alchemy. The two collaborated and found a reliable formula for porcelain with feldspar and brown Saxon clay. Production began in 1709, and in 1710, the first pieces were on sale at the Leipzig Easter Fair. These early pieces are reddish-brown and now known as Bottger stoneware.

Augustus moved the operation to Meissen, where he set up the royal porcelain factory. In Meissen, Bottger discovered, quite by accident, the soft white clay called kaolin needed to produce true white porcelain. In his book *Marks And Monograms On European And Oriental Pottery And Porcelain* William Chaffers notes:

The story is thus told: John Schnorr, a rich iron master of the Erzgebirge, in the year 1711, riding on horseback at Aue, near Schneeberg, observed that his horse's feet stuck continually into a soft white clay which impeded his progress. Hair powder for wigs, made principally

from wheat flour, was at that time in general use, and an examination of this earth suggested its substitution for the more expensive material, which was sold in large quantities at Dresden, Leipzig, and other places. Bottger used it, among others, and finding it much heavier, desired to find out the deleterious ingredients, and analyzed it, when, to his great surprise, the ingenious chemist found in it the identical properties of kaolin, which he alone required to complete his immortal discovery of true porcelain. This white earth was known in commerce by the name *Schnorrische weir Erde von Aue*. The kaolin from Aue was sent in casks sealed by dumb persons; the workmen were shut up under lock and key at Meissen as in a fortress, and the oath which they had taken to keep the secret until death was placed on the walls of the workshops. By 1713, the factory at Meissen was producing true white porcelain, and soon after they were able to add decoration using colored glazes. Encouraged by Augustus, Bottger began creating piec-

es designed by leading artists whose output rivaled the magnificent work of the Chinese.

Although Augustus never succeeded with his pursuits of alchemy, the porcelain factory at Meissen produced a fortune with what was dubbed the "white gold of Saxony." Every effort was made to prevent the secret formula—the arcanum—from falling into competitors' hands. Although the employees at Meissen were sworn to secrecy, industrial spies and defecting workmen took their knowledge of the arcanum to Vienna and Venice, laying the foundations for the European porcelain industry. Ware writes:

It is particularly interesting to note that the most artistic porcelain was produced in Germany during the lifetime of August the Strong of Saxony (1670–1733), George II of England (1683–1760), and Louis XV of France (1710–1774). The art reached its height and began to decline before Maria Theresa, Empress of

Austria (1717–1780), and Frederick the Great, King of Prussia (1712–1786) had died; a few years before George Washington became the first president of the United States (1789); and almost a half century before Napoleon (1769–1821) ruled as emperor (1804–1814).

When Augustus died in 1733, he left nine children, a kingdom in financial ruin, and a personal collection of more than thirty-five thousand pieces of porcelain. Decorative British and European tea caddies began appearing during the Rococo era (1715–1774). The Rococo movement began in Paris and was championed by Madame de Pompadour, mistress of the new King Louis XV, partly as a retort to the baroque court of Louis XIV at Versailles. The Rococo Era was characterized by lightness, elegance, scenes of courtly love, and an exuberant celebration of nature; a much simpler artistic depiction of life than the over-the-top style of Versailles. Rococo painter Jean Antoine Watteau, best known for his depictions of elegantly dressed figures gathered in outdoor spaces, exchanging pleasantries and enjoying music, inspired painters of tea caddies. Many British and Continental tea caddies in this collection were painted during the Rococo Period and remain hugely appealing today.

The term "tea caddy" now encompasses the entire realm of tea containers in all styles and materials. This collection of tea caddies represents and reflects changing trends in fashion and taste during a remarkably diverse period in world history from the late seventeenth through the nineteenth centuries.

The Renowned Collector John Sheepshanks as the Housekeeper Brings His Letters and Morning Tea. ©Victoria and Albert Museum, London

By the beginning of the eighteenth century, tea drinking in Britain had become well established, and it was known that tea had to be protected from moisture and light. The earliest tea caddies in Britain were silver in the form of a bottle with a narrow neck and pull-off lid. The tea was put into the caddy by a sliding base or sliding shoulder and dispensed through the neck. Although silver tea caddies tended to have a rectangular form, elliptical and octagonal examples also exist. In *Tea, Trade & Tea Canisters* Antonia Agnew, David Doxey, and Felicity Marno write:

> In England, following the example of Catherine of Braganza, tea became the fashionable drink among the aristocratic women, and they served it while entertaining visitors in their boudoir. Due to its high value and social cachet, ladies adopted the Dutch habit of preparing it themselves in front of their guests. It soon became apparent that to keep tea fresh it needed to be kept in an airtight container, and because of the cost of the tea, the container had to be under the supervision of the mistress of the household. One item she had readily available and that answered these criteria was the flask from her toilet service. The forms of 17th century and early 18th century silver tea canisters correspond closely with contemporary flasks from toilet services. Furthermore, it was easy for the silversmiths to adapt the flask designs into tea canisters . . . they were available, suitable and had high value and status. Square, rectangular, polygonal, lobed, and baluster with pedestal are all forms that were first made in silver and later replicated in ceramic materials.

British designs for two silver tea caddies and a small box, c. 1694. ©*Victoria and Albert Museum, London*

Two silver tea caddies: top by Bowles Nash, c.1722; bottom by Paul de Lamerie, c. 1735. Both have lead linings. ©*Victoria and Albert Museum, London*

The smaller caddies are for black and green tea. The slightly larger container is for sugar.

Set of three English Georgian tea caddies and covers, c. 1760 (TOP)

MATERIALS/DECORATION: Sterling silver sitting upon shell feet with pineapple finials.

MARK: "DS" over "RS"/"C," lion head looking at you wearing crown.

DIMENSIONS: 5¼" H × 4¼" W × 2¼" D; 5¾" H × 4¼" W × 3¼" D; 5¼" H × 4¼" W × 2¼" D

MAKER: Daniel Smith and Robert Sharp

PROVENANCE: Purchased in Edmonton, Canada, while working at the Citadel Theatre on a musical version of Robert Louis Stevenson's *Treasure Island*.

NOTES: The slightly larger container (center) is for sugar. They would probably have had a wooden, lockable chest.

English Sheffield tea caddy and cover, c. 1850–1900 (MIDDLE LEFT)

MATERIALS/DECORATION: Plated silver with raised embossed shield device, engraved "Cheline" on the top of cover.

MARK: "4/WH" within an oval; "&" within a shield; and the numbers "3305" and scratched "79591"; also to side "MP" over "A" in a styled shield form.

DIMENSIONS: 4¼" H × 3" W × 2½" D

MAKER: William Hutton (& son)

PROVENANCE: Purchased in London.

English quatrefoil tea caddy and oval cover, dated 1871 (BOTTOM LEFT)

MATERIALS/DECORATION: Sterling silver, reeded design from the bottom of the body peaks in center of front, back, and sides. On the cover there is a wavy band around the top.

MARK: On the lid: "HA," symbol of a crown, lion, and lowercase "h." Same on the base, plus hand scratched "1848," "L/S," "I/R," or "V/S" "1/R"

DIMENSIONS: 3" H × 2½" W × 1¼" D

MAKER: Sheffield

PROVENANCE: Purchased in London.

American rectangular tea caddy and cover, c. 1893–1930

MATERIALS/DECORATION: Sterling silver
MARK: Stamped "STERLING" over flying dragon over "680" scratched in "WRIX"
DIMENSIONS: 3¾" H × 3" W × 2" D
MAKER: The Merrill Shops

American Baltimore globular-shaped tea caddy and cover, c. 1899–1920

MATERIALS/DECORATION: Sterling silver, repousse landscape with castle to the front, windmill to the reverse while flowers cover the ground.
MARK: STERLING, symbol of a hand with the word "made" still visible
DIMENSIONS: 4" H × 3½" diameter
MAKER: A. G. Schultz, Baltimore, Maryland
PROVENANCE: Baltimore Antiques Show.

American ovoid-shaped tea caddy and cover, c. 1900

MATERIALS/DECORATION: Sterling silver. Undecorated.
MARK: Wright Kay & Co, sterling; "2" over a "Y" or an "I"
DIMENSIONS: 4¼" H × 3" diameter
MAKER: Wright Kay & Co
PROVENANCE: Purchased in St. Michaels, Maryland.

English tea caddy and oval cover with moving loop handles, c. 1900

MATERIALS/DECORATION: Electro-plated nickel silver
MARK: "EPNS" each within a square shield; scratched "11" under the cover
DIMENSIONS: 3" H × 3¾" W × 2¾" D
MAKER: Possibly Sheffield
PROVENANCE: Purchased in London.

English oval tea caddy with hinged cover, c. 1902

MATERIALS/DECORATION: Sterling silver
MARK: Sterling silver "made in England" on bottom,
    "BRO<<LTD" over what appears to be a stylized "M";
    symbol of an anchor, lion, and "C," each within a shield.
    On the lid, the symbol of a lion and "C"
DIMENSIONS: 4" H × 3½" W × 2" D
MAKER: Birmingham
PROVENANCE: Purchased in Philadelphia.

English Sheffield quatrefoil tea caddy and cover, dated 1903

MATERIALS/DECORATION: Sterling silver with leafy
    pendant scrolls and flower head and leaves as the central
    design, with garland of flowers to the lower half framing a
    two-headed eagle with a cover on the chest. There is a
    wave border around the top of the shoulder and the cover.
MARK: "HA" under symbol of a crown, lion, "I" or "L"
DIMENSIONS: 3¼" H × 3" W × 2" D
MAKER: Atkins Brothers
PROVENANCE: Purchased in London.

English oval tea caddy and lid, c. 1903

MATERIALS/DECORATION: Sterling silver
MARK: "CS*FS," symbol of a lion, three sheaves around a
    sword, and stylized "C" on lid
DIMENSIONS: 3¼" H × 2¼" W × 1¾" D
MAKER: Chester
PROVENANCE: Purchased in London.

American six-sided ovoid tea caddy and cover, c. 1907

MATERIALS/DECORATION: Sterling silver
    with "B" script initial.
MARK: Sterling, initials "RW," "14,14" under cover.
DIMENSIONS: 4¾" H × 3½" diameter
MAKER: Roger Williams
PROVENANCE: Purchased at J. R.'s Antiques,
    Queenstown, Maryland.

English cylindrical tea caddy and cover, c. 1908

MATERIALS/DECORATION: Sterling silver
    with no ornamentation.
MARK: "W.N." over "L" to right; symbols: anchor, lion, and "i"
DIMENSIONS: 3¾" H × 3" diameter
MAKER: William Neal
PROVENANCE: Purchased in Manchester, England, while
    there with Harold Fielding's production of *Barnum*,
    starring Michael Crawford.

English oval shaped tea caddy and cover, c. 1911

MATERIALS/DECORATION: Sterling silver repousse with
    processional scene around the lower half.
MARK: On cover: symbol lion, and a script "L." On underside
    of base: symbol lion, three sheaves, script "L" and a "25."
DIMENSIONS: 3¼" H × 3" W × 2¼" D
MAKER: Chester
PROVENANCE: Purchased in London.

Russian ovoid form tea caddy and cover, c. 1920

MATERIALS/DECORATION: Sterling silver with niello
    decoration (also known as "tula" work).
MARK: None
DIMENSIONS: 4¾" H × 2½" diameter
MAKER: Unknown
PROVENANCE: Purchased in Moscow while working
    on *42nd Street*.
NOTES: Niello is a black metallic alloy of sulfur with silver,
    copper, or lead that is used to fill designs engraved on the
    surface of an object. It is made by fusing together silver,
    copper, and lead, then mixing the molten alloy with sulfur.
    The resulting black-colored sulfides are powdered, and
    after the engraved silver is moistened with a flux, some of
    the powder is spread on it and the metal strongly heated;
    the niello melts and runs into the engraved channels. The
    excess niello is then removed by scraping until the filled
    channels are clearly visible. Finally, the surface is polished.
    The contrast of the black against the bright silver surface
    produces a handsome decorative effect.

Maryland Silver

Our great family friend Stiles T. Colwill, interior designer, former museum curator, and collector of all things Maryland, shared these tea caddies and equipage from his collection.

American, pair of Baltimore rectangular-shaped tea caddies with screw on tops, c. 1820
MATERIALS/DECORATION: Undecorated sterling silver
MARK: Signed
DIMENSIONS: 2¾" H × 2" W × 1½" D
MAKER: A. E. Warner
NOTES: These would likely have had either a leather or wooden case.

American, Baltimore basket-shaped tea caddy, c. 1800–05
MATERIALS/DECORATION: Sterling silver with hinged lid and handle
MARK: Signed
DIMENSIONS: 4¼" H × 4½" W × 4" D
MAKER: Charles Louis Boehm

American, Baltimore oval-shaped tea caddy with hinged cover, c. 1800
MATERIALS/DECORATION: Sterling silver
MARK: Signed
DIMENSIONS: 4" H × 4¾" W × 2¾" D
MAKER: Standish Barry

American, Baltimore urn-shaped tea caddy and cover, with a covered sugar box, c. 1800

MATERIALS/DECORATION: Sterling silver, with engraved initials "R.O".

MARK: Signed

DIMENSIONS: The caddy is 5¾" H × 3" diameter

MAKER: Thomas Warner

NOTES: It is interesting to see how large the sugar box is compared to the tea caddy.

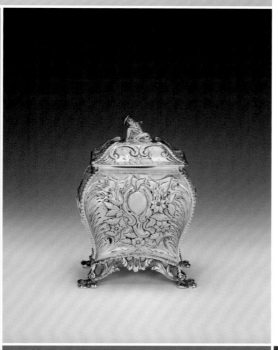

American, Baltimore chest-shaped tea caddy and cover, c. 1835

MATERIALS/DECORATION: Sterling silver embossed design to body and cover.

MARK: Signed

DIMENSIONS: 6" H × 4½" W × 3¼" D

MAKER: Andrew Warner

Sterling silver cup strainer.

Sterling silver spout strainer.

Stiles T. Colwill On Collecting Maryland Silver Tea Caddies

I started collecting Maryland silver in 1977. As a young assistant curator at the Maryland Historical Society with a love of antique silver, I thought it would be a challenge to "assemble" a harlequin tea service, consisting of a large hot water or coffee pot, a teapot or two, creamer, sugar, waste bowl, and a tea caddy. The service would consist of six or seven pieces all by different makers in a coordinating historical style. In fact, this was commissioned in the 1790s by one of Baltimore's wealthiest couples, the young Rachel Gratz of Philadelphia and her new husband Solomon Etting, who over a number of years ordered the various pieces for their service from a variety of different makers, but when set out, they all would appear to be of the same hand. Little did I know how easy part of the mission would be to accomplish, and in turn, virtually impossible to complete. The first five or six pieces were relatively easy to acquire, but now, almost forty years later, the illusive en suit tea caddy has yet to be found. Not that tea caddies cannot be had, but they are extremely rare and seemingly never matching a set. The various items for a service abound in my collection today, including one coffee urn, over thirty tea or coffee pots, thirty-two creamers, twenty-eight sugar basins or baskets, fourteen waste bowls, and five tea caddies. If one starts to research American, you will find they are very rare; Maryland tea caddies even more so. In checking the three standard references for Maryland silver, the original source, *Maryland Silversmiths 1750–1830* (Pleasants and Sill, published in 1930), only two tea caddies are discussed. The next reference, *Eighteenth and Nineteenth Century Maryland Silver in the Collection of The Baltimore Museum of Art* (Jennifer Goldsborough, published in 1975), does not list a single tea caddy. Finally, *Silver in Maryland*, an exhibition catalog by the Maryland Historical Society in 1984, only lists two tea caddies, and one of those is the same as in Pleasants and Sill's. To date, there is no record of any tea caddy matching a larger extant service, so forty years later the collection has grown and continues to grow. While I have acquired five caddies, each being very special and each appreciated for its own unique design, I have yet to find one that matched the tea service. But that is what keeps us all collecting: the elusive object, long sought after and yet to be found.

Still Life With Teapot, Teacup, Lemon, and Cherries. Author's collection

Chapter 2
CHINESE

The Chinese are credited with inventing many items we use today, including the four great inventions: paper making, the compass, gunpowder, and printing, all of which have had a profound impact all over the world. Another significant contribution from China was the invention of porcelain. Chinese inventor Tao-Yue (608–676 AD) is credited with this discovery, although it took many years to perfect. He used kaolin (called "white clay") found along the Yangtze River where he was born, added other types of clay, and produced the first white porcelain, which he sold as "artificial jade" in the capital Chang'an. His techniques for combining the proper ingredients, including the translucent feldspar and quartz, continued to evolve, and by around 900 AD, porcelain was perfected. By the time of the Sung Dynasty (960–1279 AD), porcelain had reached its artistic height and collectors throughout the world regard porcelain bowls and vases produced in the years that followed, especially during the Ming Dynasty (1368–1644), as artistic treasures. Porcelain makers mastered the ubiquitous blue and white under-glaze decoration and over-glaze painting with enamel colors during this time. In the 1100s, the secret of making porcelain had spread to Korea, and by the 1500s, to Japan. Europe saw porcelain for the first time in the mid-sixteenth century, when the first pieces were brought over by the Portuguese from their trading post on Macao. Porcelain was much thinner than other clay ceramics, so thin as to be translucent when held up to light. Its white base could be adorned in many colors. As one of the most highly prized Chinese products, it came to be known simply as "china," a term we still use today for fine dishware. From the time the first pieces of porcelain arrived in Europe, kings, scientists, and potters began searching for the recipe for true porcelain. It became known as "white gold" and remains a status symbol to this day.

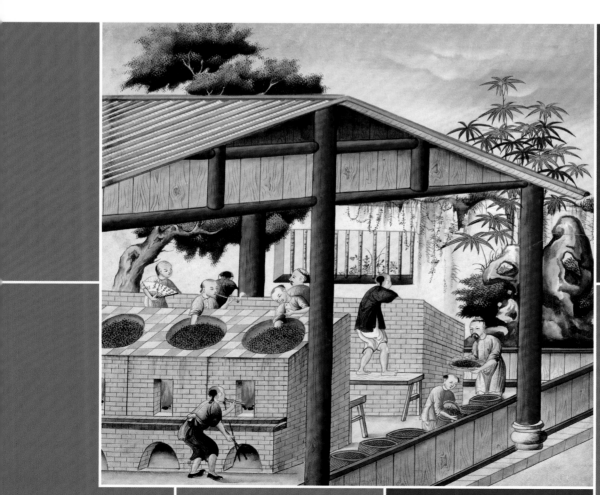

Firing tea in China, late eighteenth century. ©Victoria and Albert Museum, London

Miniature Kangxi Chinese export teapot and cover, c. 1710

MATERIALS/DECORATION: Porcelain with underglaze blue decoration.

MARK: Leaf and scroll Artemisia mark

DIMENSIONS: 2" H × 3¾" W

MAKER: Unknown

PROVENANCE: The Moog, Atlanta, while directing the 2002 National Tour of *42nd Street* at the Fox Theatre.

Chinese export Kangxi vase or bottle, c. 1710

MATERIALS/DECORATION: Porcelain with underglaze blue decoration of rocks and trees with nineteenth-century silver mounts (probably Dutch).

MARK: None

DIMENSIONS: 6¾" H × 3" diameter

MAKER: Unknown

PROVENANCE: Purchased in Holland.

Chinese export ovoid form tea caddy with silver cover, c. 1720

MATERIALS/DECORATION: Porcelain reeded body with three circular panels with Chinese precious objects in blue and white underglaze decoration and blue bat designs encircling the neck. The caddy sits upon an eighteenth-century silver band at the foot with nineteenth-century Dutch silver mount and cover.

MARK: Hallmark, four character Kangxi marks

DIMENSIONS: 6" H × 3¾" diameter

MAKER: Unknown

PROVENANCE: Purchased in Holland.

Chinese export octagonal tea caddy and associated wood cover, c. 1720–40

MATERIALS/DECORATION: Porcelain reeded body decorated with central blue panel with iron red stylized flower heads, flanking orange panels with iron red stylized flowers and gilt vines on side panels with flowering branches.

MARK: None

DIMENSIONS: 4½" H × 3¾" W × 2¼" D

MAKER: Unknown

Chinese export octagonal tea caddy and associated silver cover, c. 1740

MATERIALS/DECORATION: Porcelain with each panel decorated with iron red flower motif; shoulder similarly decorated.

MARK: None

DIMENSIONS: 3¾" H × 3" W × 1¾" D

MAKER: Unknown

PROVENANCE: Winter Antiques Show, New York.

Chinese export octagonal tea caddy, c. 1740

MATERIALS/DECORATION: Porcelain with large central panel with chrysanthemums in iron red, small panels to either side with flowers in underglaze blue. Sides decorated with spray of chrysanthemums in iron red. Traces of gilt on the mums.

MARK: None

DIMENSIONS: 4" H × 3½" W × 2" D

MAKER: Unknown

PROVENANCE: Purchased in Boston.

Chinese (I Hsing) pottery tea caddy, c.1740–80

MATERIALS/DECORATION: Red pottery with incised shields emanating from the shoulder. Two incised lines run at the base of the shoulder. Incised circles rim incised (stamped) flower upon the top of the cover.

MARK: Unmarked

DIMENSIONS: 4½" H × 3½" diameter

MAKER: Unknown

PROVENANCE: Spring Antiques Show at the Park Avenue Armory, New York.

Chinese export ovoid form tea caddy and cover, c. 1745

MATERIALS/DECORATION: Porcelain with famille rose decoration upon an applied scroll molding around the base. En grisaille floral and foliate ground to the body and cover with reserve panel to the front and reverse depicting flower arrangement upon a marble table.

MARK: Unmarked

DIMENSIONS: 5¼" H × 2⅝" diameter

MAKER: Unknown

Note how small the teapot is compared to the caddy.

Chinese export ovoid form tea caddy with dome cover and related teapot, c. 1745

MATERIALS/DECORATION: Porcelain, the body decorated with three koi fish—one in iron red and two en grisaille; bands of diaper to the shoulder and edge of the cover; relief panel with orange florets and applied scroll molding around the base.

MARK: Unmarked

DIMENSIONS: Caddy: 5¼" H × 3" diameter; teapot 5" H × 8" W

MAKER: Unknown

PROVENANCE: Caddy from The Moog, Atlanta; teapot purchased in London.

NOTES: En grisaille (deriving from the French word *gris* for gray) refers to a technique using monochromatic tones of gray and black—or in this case red—over-glaze enamel executed in fine strokes. Chinese legend tells how the Koi swam up a waterfall and were magically transformed into dragons. In the catalog for the 2002 Stockspring Antiques loan exhibition in London, Antonia Agnew, David Doxey, and Felicity Marno comment: "The scroll molding found around the base of these shapes is only found on Chinese tea canisters for export. It is possibly derived from a misinterpretation of a design for gilding sent out to China by the East India Company."

Chinese export ovoid form tea caddy and associated cover, c. 1745

MATERIALS/DECORATION: Porcelain decorated with en grisaille mythical scenes. On the front, Venus and Cupid ride through the clouds in a chariot pulled by two doves. Cupid is shooting an arrow at a resting Roman soldier (possibly Adonis) who is guarded by Minerva. Applied scroll molding around the base. Associated silver cover.

MARK: Unmarked

DIMENSIONS: 5" H × 3" diameter

MAKER: Unknown

PROVENANCE: The Moog, Atlanta.

Chinese export footed rectangular form tea caddy and cover, c. 1745

MATERIALS/DECORATION: Porcelain with en grisaille flowers accented in green and yellow. There is a lappet border beneath the shoulder.

MARK: None

DIMENSIONS: 3¼" H × 3¾" W × 2¼" D

MAKER: Unknown

PROVENANCE: Mimi's Antiques of Columbia, Maryland, at the Easton Academy of Arts & Antiques Show, Easton, Maryland.

Chinese export ovoid form tea caddy and cover, c. 1745

MATERIALS/DECORATION: Porcelain with famille rose decoration with central wicker basket and flower arrangement in gold iron-red en grisaille to the front, with scattered flowerets. On the reverse, a small table with an offering of fruit and flowers. The base has a repeating leaf-shaped diaper with flower within coin ground. Domed cover similarly decorated. Applied scroll molding around the base.

MARK: None

DIMENSIONS: 4¾" H × 2¾" diameter

MAKER: Unknown

PROVENANCE: Purchased in London.

Chinese export miniature tea caddy with cover and tea bowl with saucer, c. 1750

MATERIALS/DECORATION: Porcelain with floral and foliate famille rose decoration and gilt trim. The caddy sits upon an applied scroll wave around the base.

MARK: None

DIMENSIONS: The caddy is 3¼" H × 2" diameter; the saucer is 3" diameter

MAKER: Unknown

PROVENANCE: Stockspring Antiques, London.

Chinese export ovoid form tea caddy and associated cover, c. 1750

MATERIALS/DECORATION: Porcelain with central flowering branches and leaves decoration extending around the body. Small bird sits upon the branch, scattered insects throughout. Leaves are brown highlighted in gilt, flowers are iron red. Simple narrow-looped border where the shoulder meets the neck and applied scroll molding around the base. Silvered metal cover.

MARK: None

DIMENSIONS: 5¼" H × 3" diameter

MAKER: Unknown

Chinese export miniature ovoid tea caddy, c. 1750

MATERIALS/DECORATION: Porcelain with famille rose decoration with various flowering branches and insects resting upon applied scroll molding around the base.

MARK: Unmarked

DIMENSIONS: 2½" H × 2" diameter

MAKER: Unknown

PROVENANCE: Stockspring Antiques, London.

Chinese export ovoid form tea caddy on a flared foot, c. 1750

MATERIALS/DECORATION: Porcelain with Mandarin ducks, flowers, and plants. Lower section of the body is reeded, with lotus flowers in relief to the front and a flying duck to the reverse.

MARK: None

DIMENSIONS: 4" H × 3" diameter

MAKER: Unknown

PROVENANCE: Winter Antiques Show, New York.

Chinese export ovoid form tea caddy, c. 1755

MATERIALS/DECORATION: Porcelain with European decoration of a continuous scene of a man and woman standing in a garden; he holds a pitchfork, she a basket of flowers. On the reverse, another female figure waters roses beneath a large yellow and brown tree.

MARK: Unmarked

DIMENSIONS: 4" H × 3" diameter

MAKER: Unknown

PROVENANCE: Purchased in England.

Chinese export ovoid form tea caddy, c. 1765

MATERIALS/DECORATION: Porcelain, famille rose decoration depicting domestic scenes of two children with grandparent (in each scene) while a parent observes through a window from another room. Sides decorated with scrolling rococo cartouches framing birds. Applied scroll wave molding around the base.

MARK: Unmarked

DIMENSIONS: 4" H × 3" diameter

MAKER: Unknown

NOTES: The neck has been removed.

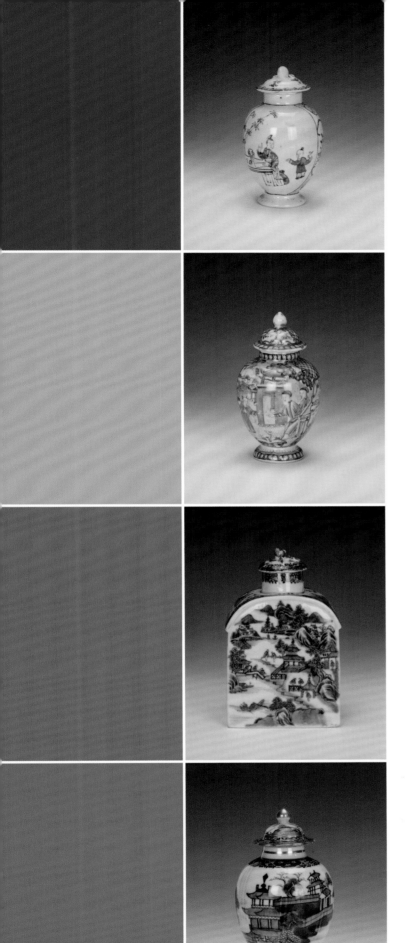

Chinese export ovoid form tea caddy upon a flared foot, c. 1765

MATERIALS/DECORATION: Porcelain with famille rose decoration depicting domestic scenes to the front and reverse. At each side there are panels with sprigs of florets within scrolling rococo cartouche. Associated cover with a melon finial.

MARK: Unmarked

DIMENSIONS: 5½" H × 3¼" diameter

MAKER: Unknown

Chinese export ovoid form tea caddy and cover, c. 1765

MATERIALS/DECORATION: Porcelain decorated in Mandarin palette of domestic scenes before a natural mountainous landscape. At the sides, black coin ground and simple iron red landscape scenes within rococo framed panels. Cover similarly decorated.

MARK: Unmarked

DIMENSIONS: 5¾" H × 3" diameter

MAKER: Unknown

PROVENANCE: David Pownall Willis, Plainfield, New Jersey.

Chinese export large rectangular sloped-shoulder tea caddy, c. 1770

MATERIALS/DECORATION: Porcelain with underglaze blue and white landscape pagoda and river that completely fill the fields on the front and reverse. Side panels have matching river scenes. Shoulder with depictions of buildings and sampans on the river. Blue diaper band around the upper shoulder, neck, and cover, which has a flower finial.

MARK: Unmarked

DIMENSIONS: 6" H × 3½" W × 2" D

MAKER: Unknown

Chinese export ovoid form tea caddy and cover, c. 1775

MATERIALS/DECORATION: Porcelain with blue and white decoration featuring buildings and figures in a landscape, highlighted with English gilding.

MARK: Unmarked

DIMENSIONS: 6" H × 3¼" diameter

MAKER: Unknown

PROVENANCE: Mimi's Antiques, Columbia, Maryland.

Chinese export ovoid form tea caddy, c. 1775

MATERIALS/DECORATION: Porcelain with molded body and famille rose decoration featuring scattered floral sprays and flower heads with an applied scroll molding around the base.

MARK: Unmarked

DIMENSIONS: 4¼" H × 3" diameter

MAKER: Unknown

Chinese export rectangular sloped-shoulder tea caddy, c. 1775

MATERIALS/DECORATION: Porcelain with underglaze blue decoration of pagodas and rivers to the body and shoulder. Highlighted with contemporary English gilding.

MARK: Unmarked

DIMENSIONS: 4½" H × 3¼" W × 1⅝" D

MAKER: Unknown

PROVENANCE: Purchased in England.

Chinese export ovoid form tea caddy upon a flared foot, c. 1775

MATERIALS/DECORATION: Molded porcelain. Decorated with flowers within scrolling bianco-sopra-bianco cartouche. Famille rose flowerets scattered across the body with blue diaper border at the neck.

MARK: Unmarked

DIMENSIONS: 4¼" H × 3¼" diameter

MAKER: Unknown

PROVENANCE: Baltimore Antiques Show.

NOTES: "Bianco-sopra-bianco" (Italian for white-on-white) is an Italian term that describes a technique using white on white decoration.

Chinese export octagonal tea caddy, c. 1775

MATERIALS/DECORATION: Porcelain with underglaze blue decoration of plants and rock work to front and back with gilt highlights; narrow panels with continuous flower and stem designs. Replacement silver top.

MARK: Unmarked

DIMENSIONS: 5" H × 4" W × 2" D

MAKER: Unknown

PROVENANCE: Challiss House, San Francisco, while there working with scenic designer Douglas W. Schmidt on *Gold Diggers*.

Chinese export miniature tea service, c. 1775–85

MATERIALS/DECORATION: Porcelain with blue enamel
flowerets with gilt motif to the body. Multiple bands,
including a wave band and beaded band accents. The set
includes teapot, cover, and stand, tea caddy with cover,
two tea bowls with saucers, sugar bowl with cover, two
coffee cups, and a spoon tray.

MARK: Unmarked

DIMENSIONS: Tea caddy is 3¼" H × 2¼" W × 1" D; teapot is
4½" H × 6 ¾" W × 3½" D

MAKER: Unknown

PROVENANCE: Stockspring Antiques, London.

NOTES: In their book *Caughley Toy Wares*, Dr. Chris Holloway
and Felicity Marno write about this, or an identical, tea
service:

This Chinese toy service is particularly interesting
because of the variety of the major pieces; note
especially the tea canister, teapot stand, and spoon
tray, shapes that are regularly found in full-sized
18th Century English porcelain, but which were not
made by Caughley in toy size, and are only extremely
rarely encountered in miniature porcelain from some
of the other 18th century factories. The characteristic
Chinese "stand-off" handle to the teapot was also used
at Caughley, but only on standard-sized items.

Chinese export footed ovoid form tea caddy, c. 1775–80

MATERIALS/DECORATION: Porcelain with underglaze blue decoration featuring buildings and figures in a landscape, highlighted with English gilding.

MARK: Unmarked

DIMENSIONS: 4¾" H × 3¼" diameter

MAKER: Unknown

PROVENANCE: Purchased in England.

Chinese export rectangular sloped-shoulder tea caddy, c. 1780

MATERIALS/DECORATION: Porcelain with underglaze blue and white decoration. Lappet shoulders, double floral motif on the front and back with floral sprays to the sides.

MARK: Unmarked

DIMENSIONS: 4½" H × 3⅜" W × 1⅝" D

MAKER: Unknown

Chinese export rectangular tea caddy with rounded shoulder, c. 1780

MATERIALS/DECORATION: Porcelain with underglaze blue featuring the coat of arms for Graham Impaling Strickland with gilt border. Wave meander beneath the shoulder, and a wide underglaze blue diaper border to the shoulder and neck.

MARK: Unmarked

DIMENSIONS: 4½" H × 3½" W × 1½" D

MAKER: Unknown

PROVENANCE: Charlton Hall Galleries, West Columbia, South Carolina.

NOTES: This caddy appears in David Sanctuary Howard's *Chinese Armorial Porcelain* (Faber and Faber, 1974).

Chinese export rectangular sloped-shoulder tea caddy and cover, c. 1780

MATERIALS/DECORATION: Porcelain with reeded body decorated with a standing vase and flower arrangement upon a table to the front and back. On the sides are precious objects with floral sprays, and purple and raspberry diaper border along the upper body. Cover similarly decorated.

MARK: Unmarked

DIMENSIONS: 5" H × 3½" W × 1½" D

MAKER: Unknown

PROVENANCE: Purchased in Bath, England, while on holiday with my parents.

Shipping Tea By Boat, c. 1780–90. ©Victoria and Albert Museum, London

Chinese export rectangular sloped-shoulder tea caddy, c. 1780

MATERIALS/DECORATION: Porcelain decorated front and back with an armorial crest featuring two lovebirds within a double laurel wreath.

MARK: Unmarked

DIMENSIONS: 4¾" H × 3¼" W × 1¾" D

MAKER: Unknown

Chinese export rectangular sloped-shoulder tea caddy, c. 1780

MATERIALS/DECORATION: Porcelain with underglaze blue Chinese pagoda and landscape continuous to both sides. With a later silvered collar and cover.

MARK: Unmarked

DIMENSIONS: 4⅝" H × 3⅛" W × 1⁷⁄₁₆" D

MAKER: Unknown

Two Chinese export octagonal-shaped tea caddies with covers, c. 1780

MATERIALS/DECORATION: Porcelain with underglaze blue featuring flowering plants (possibly a version of the "Immortelle pattern"). One caddy has an iron-colored band at the edge of the shoulder and cover.

MARK: Unmarked

DIMENSIONS: Each 4½" H × 3½" W × 2¼" D

MAKER: Unknown

PROVENANCE: William Doyle Galleries, New York.

Chinese export rectangular sloped-shoulder tea caddy with cover, c. 1780

MATERIALS/DECORATION: Porcelain with famille rose decoration. To the front and reverse an enameled panel of a lady playing the spinet before a green drape. A floral meander circles the body beneath the shoulder and upon the cover.

MARK: Unmarked

DIMENSIONS: 5½" H × 3¼" W × 1½" D

MAKER: Unknown

NOTES: Similar caddies sold at Sotheby's, New York, in 2000, and at Christie's, New York, in 2007.

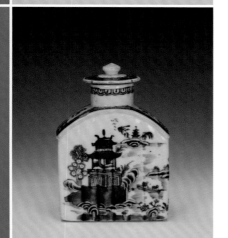

Chinese export rectangular sloped-shoulder tea caddy and cover, c. 1780

MATERIALS/DECORATION: Porcelain with molded reeded surface. Decorated in underglaze blue with a pagoda and river scene with two figures on a bridge and ornate borders to the front and reverse. At the edge of the upper shoulder is a brown-gold edge to the shoulder. The cover is flat with a button finial and fluted edge.

MARK: Unmarked

DIMENSIONS: 5" H × 3½" W × 1¾" D

MAKER: Unknown

Chinese export rectangular sloped-shoulder tea caddy, c. 1780

MATERIALS/DECORATION: Porcelain with underglaze blue decoration of a pagoda and river design to the front, reverse, and sides. Flower sprigs at the shoulder within a wide diaper ground border.

MARK: Unmarked

DIMENSIONS: 4½" H × 3½" W × 1¾" D

MAKER: Unknown

Chinese export miniature ovoid form tea caddy and cover, c. 1780

MATERIALS/DECORATION: Porcelain decorated with figures in the famille verte palette.

MARK: Faux Chinese marks

DIMENSIONS: 3" H × 2" diameter

MAKER: Unknown

PROVENANCE: Stockspring Antiques, London.

Chinese export miniature rectangular sloped-shoulder tea caddy and cover, c. 1780

MATERIALS/DECORATION: Porcelain decorated with a shield and ermine crest to the front and back. Finely gilded with intertwining foliate bands. Cover with blue enamel and gold star border.

MARK: Unmarked

DIMENSIONS: 3⅜" H × 2" W × 1" D

MAKER: Unknown

Chinese export rectangular sloped-shoulder tea caddy, c. 1780

MATERIALS/DECORATION: Porcelain decorated in overglaze enamel with the seal of the State of New York. Navy and gilt star border with an iron red chevron to the shoulder and a navy band with gilt beading to the base.

MARK: Unmarked

DIMENSIONS: 5" H × 3¼" W × 1¼" D

MAKER: Unknown

PROVENANCE: Purchased in New York.

The rectangular sloped-shoulder tea caddy was the most popular form in the eighteenth century.

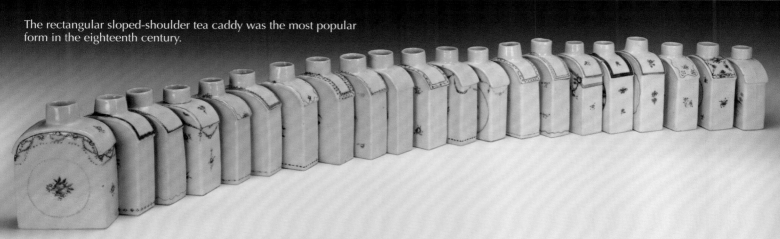

Chinese export octagonal tea caddy, c. 1780

MATERIALS/DECORATION: Porcelain with underglaze blue and white floral and foliate decoration. Later metal sleeve to the neck.

MARK: Unmarked

DIMENSIONS: 4" H × 3¼" W × 2" D

MAKER: Unknown

Chinese export rectangular sloped-shoulder tea caddy, c. 1785

MATERIALS/DECORATION: Porcelain with Mandarin decoration panels to the front and back with multiple figures within garden scenes. Side panels feature flower sprays surrounded by puce diaper ground. Scattered flowers to the shoulders.

MARK: Unmarked

DIMENSIONS: 4½" H × 3⅛" W × 1¾" D

MAKER: Unknown

PROVENANCE: Imperial Antiques, Stockport, England.

Chinese export rectangular sloped-shoulder tea caddy, c. 1790

MATERIALS/DECORATION: Porcelain decorated in blue enamel and gold armorial device to each side with the initials "RAS" draped in blue.

MARK: Unmarked

DIMENSIONS: 4¾" H × 3¼" W × 1½" D

MAKER: Unknown

PROVENANCE: Purchased in Windsor, England.

Chinese export rectangular form tea caddy, c. 1830

MATERIALS/DECORATION: Porcelain with underglaze blue decoration featuring central foliate flower head and foliate leaves within stylized cloud border to each side. Shoulder decorated with foliate flowers. Wooden cover.

MARK: Unmarked

DIMENSIONS: 6" H × 4⅜" W × 2¾" D

MAKER: Unknown

PROVENANCE: Mimi's Antiques of Columbia, Maryland, at the Easton Academy of Arts & Antiques Show, Easton, Maryland.

Chinese export large hexagonal tea caddy and cover, c. 1830–40

MATERIALS/DECORATION: Pale blue body with underglaze blue featuring Nanking Chinese landscape.

MARK: Four Chinese marks.

DIMENSIONS: 6¼" H × 5" circumference

MAKER: Unknown

PROVENANCE: Auction at Russum's Antiques, Crumpton, Maryland.

Chinese five-sided flower-shaped tea caddy, c. 1850–70

MATERIALS/DECORATION: Porcelain with underglaze blue stylized flower surrounded by foliate scrolls. Curl-work border to the upper body and the shoulder.

MARK: Unmarked

DIMENSIONS: 5¼" H × 4" circumference

MAKER: Unknown

PROVENANCE: De accession from the National Museum Of China. Purchased in Beijing while in China directing *42nd Street*.

Chinese export rectangular tea caddy, c. 1820

MATERIALS/DECORATION: Molded porcelain with blue Asian character surrounded by a scroll and flower device to the front and reverse. A raised blue border surrounds the rectangular panels. Panels to the sides with dual Chinese symbols surrounded by scrollwork.

MARK: Unmarked

DIMENSIONS: 4⅞" H × 3⅝" W × 1⅞" D

MAKER: Unknown

Chinese red ware cylindrical tea caddy and cover, c. nineteenth century

MATERIALS: Zisha clay

MARK: Unmarked

DIMENSIONS: 4" H × 3" diameter

MAKER: Unknown

NOTES: Zisha pottery has existed for 500 to 600 years. Zisha clay is only found in the Wolong mountains near Yixing, China, and is used to create a kind of stoneware that falls somewhere between pottery and porcelain. In the Tang Dynasty (618–907 AD) tea drinking gained acceptance as a beverage, and in the Song Dynasty (960–1279 AD) tea consumption blossomed. During this time tea was stored in bricks known as "tea cakes," which were ground and powdered, then scooped into a tea bowl and whisked until frothy. In the Ming Dynasty (1368–1644 AD), Emperor Zhu Yuanzhang preferred the tender buds of earliest spring tea steeped in a teapot and abolished "tea cakes." It is from this time that we find Zisha teapots. From the seventeenth century forward Yixing wares were commonly exported to Europe.

Chinese export square base tea caddy, c. nineteenth century

MATERIALS/DECORATION: Porcelain with later wooden cover. Underglaze blue floral and foliate design in the slightly recessed panels and to the shoulder.

MARK: Unmarked

DIMENSIONS: 5¾" H × 3½" W × 3½" D

MAKER: Unknown

Pair of Chinese globular-form tea caddies, c. 1860–1900

MATERIALS/DECORATION: Porcelain with underglaze blue decoration of vines surrounding the front and back and blue fence design. Bands of clouds beneath the shoulder, one which starts at the base of the neck. Chinese character device to either side.

MARK: Unmarked

DIMENSIONS: 4¼" H × 4⅜" diameter

MAKER: Unknown

Chinese hexagonal pottery tea caddy, c. twentieth century

MATERIALS/DECORATION: Redware pottery, stamped stylized line badges on each side and on the deep shoulders.

MARK: Unmarked

DIMENSIONS: 5" H × 4¼" at base, 5½" at shoulder

MAKER: Unknown

Miniature Chinese teapot and cover, c. 1920

MATERIALS/DECORATION: Porcelain with en grisaille decoration featuring a landscape and Chinese characters. Chinese symbol beneath the spout and to the top of the cover.

MARK: Unmarked

DIMENSIONS: 3" H × 5¼" across × 3" diameter

MAKER: Unknown

Chapter 3
GERMAN

Augustus The Strong led the German search to discover the formula (arcanum) for manufacturing true porcelain. Around 1710, Johann Fredrich Bottger's use of feldspar, a key ingredient for porcelain, paved the way for "Bottger stoneware," a line of elegant red stoneware that set forth a significant evolution in the quality and production of German porcelain. After discovering the technique of using kaolin as a base, the factory at Meissen was producing true white porcelain by 1713. The earliest Meissen tea caddy in this collection dates to 1720, but Meissen caddies can be found as early as 1710.

Tea Time On The Terrace, Dudley Hardy. *Author's collection*

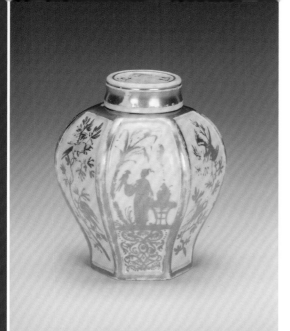

German hexagonal tea caddy and cover, c. 1720

MATERIALS/DECORATION: Bottger porcelain decorated in gilt at Augsburg, in the Seuter workshop, with alternating panels of birds and chinoiserie figures on strapwork pediments, the cover with a wide band of gilding and a bird on a branch.

MARK: Gilt "X" under the cover

DIMENSIONS: 4¼" H × 3" diameter.

MAKER: Bottger Meissen

PROVENANCE: Estate of Charlton M. Theus Jr. at Stair Galleries, Hudson, New York.

NOTES: The Seuter workshop was in Augsburg, southern Germany, an important center of printing, textile making, metalworking, and glass making. Four Seuter brothers worked in the family studio: Bartholomäus (1678–1754), Johann Paulus (1680–1735), Johannes (1686–1719), and Abraham (1689–1747). All of the brothers were skilled goldsmiths. In the early years Meissen commissioned the Seuter brothers to add gilt decoration to its wares. Although a few signed pieces by Abraham Seuter are known, most Seuter-decorated porcelains can only be ascribed to the workshop and not to the hand of any specific brother.

German rectangular sloped-shoulder tea caddy, c. 1740–45

MATERIALS/DECORATION: Porcelain with painted panels of theatricals in costume, one riding a donkey beating a drum, set in a country landscape. A dog is with them.

MARK: Underglaze blue crossed swords in brackets (obscured)

DIMENSIONS: 4" H × 2¾" W × 1¾" D

MAKER: Meissen

PROVENANCE: Stair Galleries, Hudson, New York.

German rectangular sloped-shoulder tea caddy, c. 1745

MATERIALS/DECORATION: Porcelain with underglaze Deutsche Blumen bouquets to front and back, scattered flowers to the sides.

MARK: Underglaze blue mark that cannot be read and a scratch "2"

DIMENSIONS: 4" H × 2¾" W × 1¾" D

MAKER: Unknown, attributed to Meissen

PROVENANCE: Purchased in Berlin.

German rectangular tea caddy, c. 1745

MATERIALS/DECORATION: Porcelain with associated eighteenth century gilt cover. Scenes from the commedia dell'arte, with Pierrot serenading Columbina to the front; on the reverse are two figures dancing. On each side there is a single musician standing. Wonderful painting.

MARK: Faint crossed swords underglaze blue, a gilt "7", and an incised "19"

DIMENSIONS: 4⅜" H × 3⅛" W × 1¾" D

MAKER: Meissen

PROVENANCE: Stockspring Antiques, London.

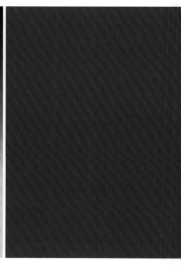

German rectangular domed basket weave shoulder tea caddy, c. 1750

MATERIALS/DECORATION: Molded porcelain painted with fruit and insects to the front and pea pod and insects to the reverse, with mushrooms and insects to one side and fruit and insects to the other. Replacement metal top.

MARK: Underglaze blue crossed swords

DIMENSIONS: 5½" H × 2¾" W × 2" D

MAKER: Meissen

PROVENANCE: Purchased in Berlin.

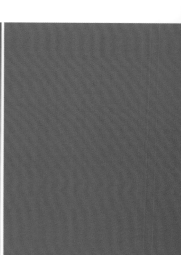

German Thuringen rectangular sloped-shoulder tea caddy, c. 1750

MATERIALS/DECORATION: Decorated in enamels with butterflies and flowers on the front and back. Scattered flowers on the shoulders.

MARK: Unmarked

DIMENSIONS: 4¼" H × 3" W × 2" D

MAKER: Unknown

PROVENANCE: Purchased in Berlin.

German rectangular sloped-shoulder tea caddy, c. mid-eighteenth century

MATERIALS/DECORATION: Porcelain with underglaze blue "Rock and Bird" Pattern. White body.

MARK: Underglaze blue crossed swords with dot and "4" on the collar

DIMENSIONS: 4⅛" H × 2⅞" W × 1⅞" D

MAKER: Meissen

South German octagonal shaped tea caddy, c. mid-eighteenth century

MATERIALS/DECORATION: Faience with alternating panels of blue ground with three flower heads against white ground with blue flower and leaves pendant.

MARK: Unmarked

DIMENSIONS: 5¼" H × 2¾" diameter

MAKER: Unknown

PROVENANCE: Purchased in Berlin.

German rectangular sloped-shoulder tea caddy, c. mid-eighteenth century

MATERIALS/DECORATION: Porcelain with botanical and fruit decoration to all four sides and a purple pendant triangle around the base of the neck. There is a butterfly to one of the side panels.

MARK: Unmarked

DIMENSIONS: 4" H × 2¾" W × 1¾" D

MAKER: Possibly Meissen

German rectangular sloped-shoulder tea caddy and cover, c. 1760

MATERIALS/DECORATION: Porcelain painted with large orange flower to front and back and smaller sprays to the sides beneath a peach ground Vandyke shoulder. Cover similarly decorated with flower finial.

MARK: Mark on base, scratch "NO 2"; script "F" to neck

DIMENSIONS: 5" H × 2¾" W × 1¾" D

MAKER: Furstenberg

PROVENANCE: Purchased in Centreville, Maryland.

A pair of German rectangular sloped-shoulder tea caddies, c. 1760

MATERIALS/DECORATION: Porcelain with reeded bodies and underglaze blue and white "straw flower" design decoration.

MARKS: One with crossed swords and a "Z" on the base of the neck; shoulder impressed with "64" on the underside. Second has crossed swords and "3" on the base of the neck/shoulder.

DIMENSIONS: 4¼" H × 2¾" W × 1⅞" D

MAKER: Meissen

German rectangular sloped-shoulder tea caddy, c. 1760

MATERIALS/DECORATION: Porcelain with reeded body decorated in underglaze blue and white with "straw flower" design, flowers, and leaves. Replacement metal cover.

MARK: None

DIMENSIONS: 4¾" H × 2¾" W × 1⅞" D

MAKER: Unknown

PROVENANCE: Phantom SF Gallery, San Francisco, while directing *42nd Street*. Purchased for a sum, plus two opening night tickets at the Orpheum Theatre.

Pair of German rectangular sloped-shoulder tea caddies, c. 1760

MATERIALS/DECORATION: Porcelain with reeded body, decorated with a variation of the "Immortelle" pattern.

MARK: None.

DIMENSIONS: 4¼" H × 2¾" W × 1¾" D

MAKER: Unknown

PROVENANCE: Purchased in Baden-Baden, Germany, on the way to meet David Merrick and Michael Stewart in the south of France.

German rectangular sloped-shoulder tea caddy, c. 1760

MATERIALS/DECORATION: Porcelain with reeded body, decorated in underglaze blue variation of the "Immortelle" pattern. Later improvised cover with cork.

MARK: None

DIMENSIONS: 4½" H × 3" W × 2" D

MAKER: Berlin

Blue-and-white German caddies. The "Immortelle," "rock and bird," and "straw flower" patterns were very popular.

German cylindrical shaped tea caddy and cover, c. 1760–70

MATERIALS/DECORATION: Porcelain with central scene of sheep and goat in a country landscape; flower heads and minute insects scattered over the body covering firing flaws in the porcelain. Teal and puce ribbon meander to the upper body and shoulder. Scattered puce flowers to the shoulder; the cover with miniature puce flowers.

MARK: Wheel and electoral crown

DIMENSIONS: 5¼" H × 3" diameter

MAKER: Hochst

PROVENANCE: Purchased from porcelainbiz.com, Sparta, New Jersey.

German rectangular sloped-shoulder tea caddy and cover, c. 1775

MATERIALS/DECORATION: Porcelain with puce flower sprays to all sides.

MARK: Underglaze blue crossed swords

DIMENSIONS: 4¼" H × 2¾" W × 1¾" D

MAKER: Meissen

German ovoid shaped tea caddy and cover, c. 1765–1800

MATERIALS/DECORATION: Porcelain decorated to each side with naturalistically rendered birds in a tree. Rococo pendant triangle gilt work to the shoulder and the rim of the domed cover.

MARK: "M3"

DIMENSIONS: 5¾" H × 3½" diameter

MAKER: Nymphenburg

PROVENANCE: Porter Davis Antiques, Seattle, Washington, while there directing *42nd Street*.

NOTES: After his accession in 1745, Maximillian III Joseph, Prince-Elector of Bavaria, ordered the creation of manufacturing companies to bail out the state finances. One of those companies, the Nymphenburg Porcelain Manufactory, was established in 1747, and is still in business today. At Nymphenberg Palace there is the Nymphenburg Porcelain Museum. The cool beauty of German hard paste porcelain was unrivaled.

German rectangular sloped-shoulder tea caddy, c. 1765

MATERIALS/DECORATION: Porcelain with very brightly painted exotic bird standing in a landscape to the front. The reverse has a bird resting on a flower stem. Beautifully painted with insects on the shoulders and side panels.

MARK: Unmarked

DIMENSIONS: 4" H × 2¾" W × 1¾" D

MAKER: Possibly Meissen

PROVENANCE: Purchased in Houston, Texas, while at the University of Houston staging a developmental production of *Fat Pig*.

German rectangular sloped-shoulder tea caddy, c. 1770

MATERIALS/DECORATION: Porcelain with central Deutsche Blumen bouquet to the front with smaller sprays to the reverse and sides. Scroll detail along the edge of the shoulder terminating in pendants at each corner.

MARK: Underglaze "F"

DIMENSIONS: 4¼" H × 2¾" W × 1¾" D

MAKER: Furstenberg

PROVENANCE: Purchased in Stuttgart, Germany.

German rectangular sloped-shoulder tea caddy, c. 1770

MATERIALS/DECORATION: Porcelain reeded body with large floral Deutsche Blumen bouquet on both sides, with small spray to each side and on each upper shoulder. Beautifully painted.

MARK: Underglaze blue "W" to the shoulder

DIMENSIONS: 4¼" H × 3" W × 2" D

MAKER: Wallendorf

PROVENANCE: Purchased in New York.

German rectangular sloped-shoulder tea caddy and cover, c. 1775

MATERIALS/DECORATION: Porcelain with well-painted puce floral bouquets on the front and back and small flower sprays to the sides and top of the shoulders. The cover features floral sprays, finial edged in puce, and applied green leaves.

MARK: Crossed swords and star with a dash for the Marcolini period

DIMENSIONS: 4⅞" H × 2⅝" W × 1⅞" D

MAKER: Meissen

PROVENANCE: Purchased in New York.

NOTES: The Marcolini period at Meissen takes its name from Count Camillo Marcolini, prime minister of the German kingdom of Saxony, where the Meissen factory was located. He was named director of the Meissen works in 1774, a position he held until 1814. Marcolini perfected the Neo-Classical style of Meissen forms and decoration. Pieces from the Marcolini period are marked with the traditional underglaze blue crossed swords, plus a star (sometimes looking like an asterisk) near the short ends of the swords.

German rectangular sloped-shoulder tea caddy and cover, c. 1775

MATERIALS/DECORATION: Molded porcelain with osier
    mold to the top of the body and wave mold to the rest of
    the body; painted bouquets of roses to the front and tulips
    to the reverse. The sides feature smaller floral sprays; the
    cover is similarly decorated with a purple tulip finial.

MARK: None

DIMENSIONS: 5½" H × 3" W × 1¾" D

MAKER: Possibly Limbach

PROVENANCE: Purchased from porcelainbiz.com, Sparta,
    New Jersey.

German rectangular sloped-shoulder tea caddy, c. 1780

MATERIALS/DECORATION: Porcelain with large well-
    painted flower spray to the front and reverse with smaller
    floral sprays to each side and to the shoulder. Replacement
    gilt cover.

MARK: Underglaze blue crossed swords and star underneath.
    Drawn/written "66" in black.

DIMENSIONS: 5" H × 2¾" W × 2" D

MAKER: Meissen, during the Marcolini period

PROVENANCE: Nikolaus Hanselman Antiques,
    Stuttgart, Germany.

German "ginger jar" form tea caddy and cover, c. 1780

MATERIALS/DECORATION: Porcelain decorated with puce leaves and flowers to the body. The cover has a puce floral scroll band, scattered flowers, and a flower finial.

MARK: Meissen crossed swords and star for the Marcolini period.

DIMENSIONS: 4½" H × 3¾" diameter

MAKER: Meissen

PROVENANCE: Purchased from porcelainbiz.com, Sparta, New Jersey.

German cylindrical tea caddy, c. 1776

MATERIALS/DECORATION: Porcelain painted front and reverse with large flower bouquets, scattered flowers to the body and shoulder, with gilt bands at the top, bottom, and shoulder.

MARK: Underglaze blue crossed swords with an "A", gilder's mark 115

DIMENSIONS: 3⅝" H × 3" diameter

MAKER: Meissen, during the Marcolini period

German rectangular sloped-shoulder tea caddy and cover, c. 1780

MATERIALS/DECORATION: Porcelain with a landscape at the front in the middle ground; to the reverse, a church and ruined building in a landscape with a figure approaching the buildings. There are trees to the side panels; the replacement cover has flowerets and a gold pinecone finial.

MARK: "N" and "2" on the bottom. At the neck "F".

DIMENSIONS: 5" H × 2¾" W × 1¾" D

MAKER: Furstenberg

PROVENANCE: Purchased from porcelainbiz.com, Sparta, New Jersey.

German rectangular sloped-shoulder tea caddy, c. 1780

MATERIALS/DECORATION: Porcelain with floral bouquets to the front and back with sprays on the sides. Married silvered metal and cork stopper with abstract floral design finial. Gilded tongue border to the edge of the shoulder.

MARK: Unmarked

DIMENSIONS: 4½" H × 2¾" W × 1⅞" D

MAKER: Possibly Meissen

PROVENANCE: Purchased in Baden-Baden, Germany.

German rectangular sloped-shoulder tea caddy, c. 1780

MATERIALS/DECORATION: Porcelain featuring exquisitely painted bouquets to the front and reverse with flower sprays to the sides with small floral spray and scattered leaf to the top of the shoulder.

MARK: Puce painted mark (looks like a script "A" and "D" merged)

DIMENSIONS: 4⅝" H × 2⅞" W × 2" D

MAKER: Thuringen

PROVENANCE: Hannelore Ploetz-Peters Antiques, Berlin, Germany.

German square tea caddy with rounded shoulders and cover, c. 1780

MATERIALS/DECORATION: Porcelain featuring a church within a landscape on the front with trees and a mountain in the distance, the reverse with two houses in a Mediterranean style landscape framed by a tree in the foreground. Gilt trim at the shoulder and around the bottom edge of the cover.

MARK: Two long and one short line intersecting with a diamond at one end

DIMENSIONS: 4¼" H × 2⅛" W × 2⅛" D

MAKER: Volkstedt

PROVENANCE: Purchased from porcelainbiz.com, Sparta, New Jersey.

German rectangular sloped-shoulder tea caddy, c. 1780

MATERIALS/DECORATION: Porcelain with underglaze blue "Immortelle" or "straw flower" pattern. Very deep color.

MARK: Crossed swords and "F"

DIMENSIONS: 4½" H × 3¼" W × 2¼" D

MAKER: Furstenberg

PROVENANCE: Purchased on Portobello Road, London.

German rectangular sloped-shoulder tea caddy, c. 1780

MATERIALS/DECORATION: Porcelain decorated in underglaze blue variation on the "Immortelle" pattern

MARK: Blue scepter and "W"

DIMENSIONS: 4¼" H × 3¼" W × 1¾" D

MAKER: Berlin

German rectangular sloped-shoulder tea caddy and cover, c. 1780

MATERIALS/DECORATION: Porcelain with Deutsche Blumen to the front and reverse with smaller sprays to each side. Associated dome cover with molded flower finial and reeded sides with flower sprays.

MARK: Unmarked

DIMENSIONS: 5" H × 2¾" W × 2" D

MAKER: Possibly Furstenberg

PROVENANCE: Purchased in Berlin.

German rectangular sloped-shoulder tea caddy and cover, c. 1780

MATERIALS/DECORATION: Porcelain reeded body decorated in underglaze blue with variation of the "Immortelle" pattern. Cover similarly decorated with a lotus finial.

MARK: Blue scepter

DIMENSIONS: 5½" H × 3" W × 2" D

MAKER: Berlin

PROVENANCE: Seidel U. Sohn Antiques, Berlin, Germany.

German rectangular sloped-shoulder tea caddy and cover, c. 1780

MATERIALS/DECORATION: Porcelain with reeded body decorated in puce. The front has a basket of flowers and flower sprays entwining themselves around the remaining three sides. The cover has a silver mount and chain attaching it to the body.

MARK: Underglaze crossed swords and star

DIMENSIONS: 5¼" H × 2¾" W × 2" D

MAKER: Meissen, during the Marcolini period

PROVENANCE: Purchased in Centreville, Maryland.

German rectangular sloped-shoulder tea caddy and cover, c. 1780–90

MATERIALS/DECORATION: Porcelain with reeded body featuring a blue underglaze decoration of flower garlands and pendant design to top and all sides.

MARK: Unmarked

DIMENSIONS: 5¼" H × 3" W × 2¼" D

MAKER: Thuringen

PROVENANCE: Stockspring Antiques, London; Robert McPherson, London.

NOTES: This caddy was exhibited in the 2002 Tea, Trade And Tea Cannisters exhibition at Stockspring Antiques, London, appearing in the catalog for that event (number 94).

German rectangular sloped-shoulder tea caddy and cover, c. 1780–90

MATERIALS/DECORATION: Porcelain with puce camaieu floral sprays to the front and reverse, sprays to the sides, and shoulder. Ornate gilt border beneath the gilt-edged shoulder. Cover similarly decorated, topped by a stylized gilt flower.

MARK: Script "G"

DIMENSIONS: 5¾" H × 3¼" W × 1¾" D

MAKER: Gera Porcelain Factory

PROVENANCE: Stockspring Antiques, London.

NOTES: Camaieu is a painting technique that uses two or three tints of a single color to create a monochromatic image with a sense of depth. This caddy was exhibited in the 2002 Tea, Trade And Tea Cannisters exhibition at Stockspring Antiques, London, appearing in the catalog of that event (number 101).

German rectangular sloped-shoulder tea caddy and associated wooden cover, c. 1780–90

MATERIALS/DECORATION: Porcelain with reeded body and underglaze blue decoration of simple flowers and garlands to the four sides and leaf sprigs to the shoulder.

MARK: Unmarked

DIMENSIONS: 4¼" H × 27⁄8" W × 2" D

MAKER: Unknown

German rectangular sloped-shoulder tea caddy, c. 1780–1800

MATERIALS/DECORATION: Porcelain decorated in blue and white featuring a bird sitting in a tree above a rock. Blue band beneath the shoulder.

MARK: None

DIMENSIONS: 4" H × 2¾" W × 1¾" D

MAKER: Thuringen

German cylindrical molded tea caddy, c. 1790

MATERIALS/DECORATION: Porcelain molded with neoclassical decoration of putti, dogs, sheep, urns, and birds. Reeded bands of aquamarine with fine gilt border and beaded raspberry dots frame the base and shoulder. Insects and flowerets scattered throughout.

MARK: Underglaze blue scepter

DIMENSIONS: 3½" H × 2⅝" diameter

MAKER: Royal Berlin

PROVENANCE: Purchased on icollector.com.

German rectangular sloped-shoulder tea caddy, c. 1800

MATERIALS/DECORATION: Porcelain with osier-molded
shoulder and large floral bouquets to the front and reverse
with smaller sprays to the sides.

MARK: Underglaze blue scepter

DIMENSIONS: 4¼" H × 3" W × 2" D

MAKER: Royal Berlin

PROVENANCE: Purchased in Chicago, Illinois.

German rectangular sloped-shoulder tea caddy and cover, c. 1800

MATERIALS/DECORATION: White molded porcelain with
raised Prunus decoration on the body and cover.

MARK: Underglaze blue scepter, three scratch marks
to one corner

DIMENSIONS: 5½" H × 3" W × 1¹⁵⁄₁₆" D

MAKER: Royal Berlin

PROVENANCE: Purchased in Berlin, while there with Roger
Kirk, costume designer for *42nd Street*.

German rectangular sloped-shoulder tea caddy and cover, c. 1870

MATERIALS/DECORATION: Porcelain decorated with
scattered strawberries, bees, and various insects to
the front, back, sides, and shoulder. A dotted gilt band
edges the shoulder. Associated cover with gilt band
and fruit finial.

MARK: Underglaze blue "F" beneath a crown; initials "GvF"
on the front panel

DIMENSIONS: 5" H × 2¾" W × 1⅝" D

MAKER: Furstenberg

German square tea caddy and domed cover, c. 1880

MATERIALS/DECORATION: Porcelain with a polychrome
flower bouquet to the front and back. The molded body
and domed cover are highlighted in gilt, with scattered
flowers to the sides, shoulder, and cover.

MARK: Unmarked

DIMENSIONS: 6½" H × 3" W × 3" D

MAKER: Unknown

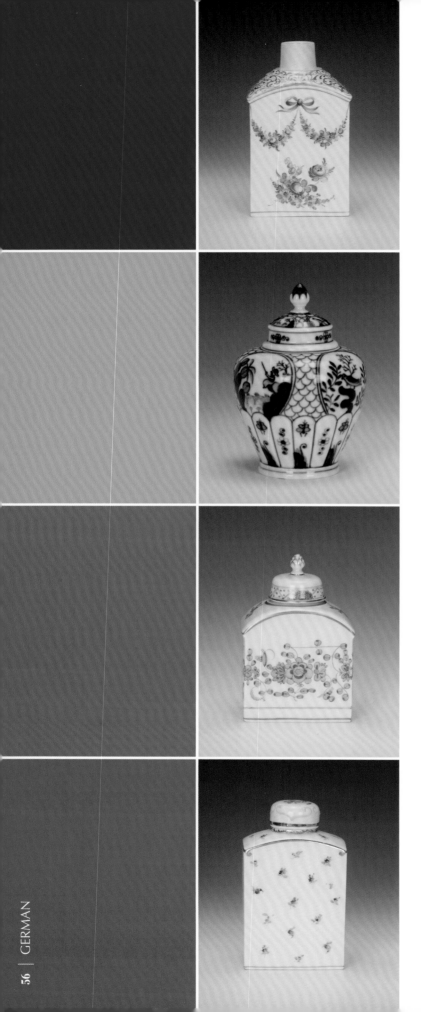

German rectangular tea caddy with sloped-shoulder, c. 1880

MATERIALS/DECORATION: Porcelain with floral swags suspended from blue bows to the upper body and flower bouquet to the lower body on all sides. The shoulder has a gilt scroll ground.

MARK: Script Dresden impressed "62" and an impressed "2"

DIMENSIONS: 6" H × 3½" W × 2¼" D

MAKER: Unknown

German baluster-shaped tea caddy and cover, c. 1880

MATERIALS/DECORATION: Porcelain decorated in underglaze blue and white chinoiserie subjects of two panels to the front and reverse of men fishing, two panels of a bird in a tree to either side. Lower section with reeded leaf design; remaining ground covered in fish scales.

MARK: Underglaze blue crossed swords, painter's mark "71" in blue

DIMENSIONS: 4½" H × 3" diameter

MAKER: Meissen

PROVENANCE: Purchased in Germany.

German diminutive sloped-shoulder tea caddy and cover, c. 1890

MATERIALS/DECORATION: Porcelain with enthusiastic puce floral decoration surrounding the body, gilt edging to the bottom, shoulder, neck, and cover. Gilt pineapple finial.

MARK: Underglaze blue crossed swords and raspberry "SVB" or "5VB" "45"

DIMENSIONS: 3⅝" H × 2⅜" W × 1⅜" D

MAKER: Meissen

PROVENANCE: Purchased on Portobello Road, London.

German rectangular sloped-shoulder tea caddy and cover, c. 1890

MATERIALS/DECORATION: Porcelain with flower heads scattered over the body and shoulder. Cover decorated with a single flower head and "bianco-sopra-bianco" detail. Gilt bands accent the base, shoulders, and cover. Gilt garland at the base of the neck.

MARK: Crown sits atop reverse "R" "K" and in script, "Dresden/Germany"

DIMENSIONS: 5½" H × 3¼" W × 2" D

MAKER: Unknown

Diminutive German rectangular sloped-shoulder tea caddy, c. nineteenth century

MATERIALS/DECORATION: Porcelain decorated with grape vines, leaves, and tendrils beneath; the shoulder is edged in gilt.

MARK: Underglaze blue crossed swords with three scratch marks

DIMENSIONS: 2¾" H × 2¼" W × 1¼" D

MAKER: Meissen

German rectangular sloped-shoulder tea caddy and cover, c. 1900

MATERIALS/DECORATION: Porcelain with a dark blue ground. Front panel depicting neoclassical rendering of "Eloisa" with putti in a beaded gilt surround. Ornate flat and raised gilt trellising to either side; gilt trellis ground to shoulder and cover. Reverse with a basket of flowers within an ornate rococo trellising surround.

MARK: Eloisa; Dresden mark with "H" in triangle

DIMENSIONS: 6" H × 2¾" W × 2" D

MAKER: Dresden

PROVENANCE: Purchased in London.

German square tea caddy, c. 1900

MATERIALS/DECORATION: Porcelain with alternating panels of flower bouquets and stylized Georgian courting couples. Gilt scrolls to the shoulder and gilt bands at the base, pendant borders to the shoulder, and with gilt at the neck.

MARK: Stamped lamb with Dresden underneath

DIMENSIONS: 5¼" H × 3 ¾" W × 3¾" D

MAKER: Dresden

German hipped rectangular tea caddy and cover, c. 1900

MATERIALS/DECORATION: Porcelain with landscapes to the front and reverse, bright gold edges at the base, shoulder, cap, and neck. Decorated in the Meissen style.

MARK: "Dresden" in script beneath stylized letters

DIMENSIONS: 4⅞" H × 3⅜" W × 2⅛" D

MAKER: Dresden

Chapter 4

ENGLISH

More tea is drunk in England than anywhere else in the world; it is considered the national beverage. By the middle of the eighteenth century, tea had become the preferred beverage among all classes in Britain and a booming business in tea equipage emerged. This is perhaps why there are so many British tea caddies.

Two Ladies and an Officer Seated at Tea, English school, c.1715.
©Victoria and Albert Museum, London

Stoneware

As in Germany, from the time the first pieces of porcelain arrived in Europe in the mid-sixteenth century, potters and scientists in England, and the rest of Europe, worked to discover the formula. Although true white porcelain was being produced in Meissen by 1713, it would be another fifty years before the formula was independently discovered in England and France. In England, one of the first significant innovations of the eighteenth century was white salt-glazed stoneware. The North Staffordshire potters had manufactured brown salt-glazed stoneware in the late seventeenth century using local clays tempered with sand. The similarity to German products of the same era suggests the influence of immigrant potters. Because they are rich in iron oxide, the Staffordshire clays fire to an orange-red color. White salt-glazed stoneware was made possible by importing clays from Devon and Dorset that had very little iron oxide in them and were white when fired. Flint was another imported material that was essential in manufacturing white salt-glazed stoneware. When mixed with the potter's clay, flint acted as a temper in the high-temperature firings necessary in the production of stoneware, with the added advantage of making the pottery more durable and whitening the body. Salt from Cheshire was a third imported ingredient that was added to the kiln during the highest temperature part of the firing process. The sodium from the salt reacts with silica in the clay to form a glassy coating of sodium silicate. The earliest examples appeared around 1720, and continued to be made throughout the eighteenth century. At the same time this fine-grained clay came into use, so did plaster molds. By 1740, press-molded salt-glazed white stoneware was all the rage, securing the reputation of the Staffordshire potters at home and abroad. An entry in the June 2013 edition of Steve Earps' blog *This Day In Pottery History* reports:

> George Washington bought hefty batches of fashionable English salt glazed white stoneware through his purchasing agent Thomas Knox in Bristol long before an independent America eclipsed Britain as the top importer of Chinese porcelain. One of Washington's orders was for "6 dozen 'finest white stone plates,' 1 dozen 'finest dishes in 6 different sizes,' 48 'patty pans' in 4 sizes, 12 butter dishes, and 12 mustard pots, plus mugs, teapots, slop basins, etc."

Salt-glazed white stoneware continued to be made throughout the eighteenth century and enjoyed tremendous popularity until interest was usurped by the invention of creamware in the mid-1740s.

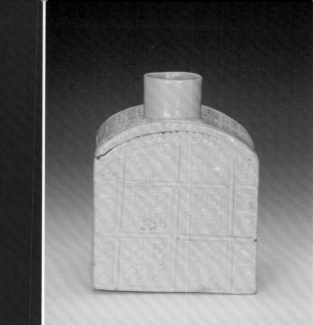

English large rectangular sloped-shoulder tea caddy, c. 1745

MATERIALS/DECORATION: Salt-glazed stoneware with press molded design of dots and stars within rope work panels. Unusually the sides, bottom, and shoulder are similarly decorated. A herringbone pattern borders where the body and shoulders meet.

MARK: Unmarked

DIMENSIONS: 4⅝" H × 3½" W × 2¾" D

MAKER: Unknown

PROVENANCE: The Winter Antiques Show, New York.

NOTES: There is extensive separation along the seams that would have occurred during firing, making this an interesting academic example.

Pair of English rectangular tea caddies, c. 1745–50

MATERIALS/DECORATION: Salt-glazed stoneware with press molded designs of dots and stars within rope work panels.

MARK: Unmarked

DIMENSIONS: 3⅝" H × 2⅜" W × 2" D

MAKER: Unknown

PROVENANCE: Sotheby's, New York; collection of Dorothy W. and F. Otto Haas; Freeman's Auction, Philadelphia, May 25, 2011, lot 49.

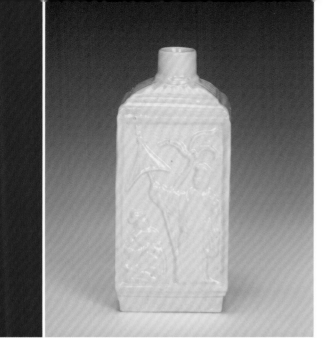

English diminutive flask form tea caddy with rounded shoulder, c. 1750

MATERIALS/DECORATION: Salt-glazed stoneware four-sided form with molded panels to each side, chinoiserie inspired design to the front and reverse, and each side with a floral and foliate scroll. Reeding to the rounded shoulder.

MARK: Unmarked

DIMENSIONS: 4" H × 1⅝" W × 1¼" D

MAKER: Unknown

PROVENANCE: Jonathan Horne of London at the New York Ceramics & Glass Fair.

English teapot and cover resting upon three lion mask and paw feet, c. 1750

MATERIALS/DECORATION: Salt-glazed stoneware molded with applied ornate sprigging, pendant band of flowers and scrolls issuing from the neck, each side with a central flower head surrounded by floral scrolls. Loop twig finial to the cover.

MARK: Unmarked

DIMENSIONS: 4¼" H × 6¾" W × 3¾" D

MAKER: Unknown

PROVENANCE: Reichner Antiques of Wilmette, Illinois, at the Baltimore Antiques Show.

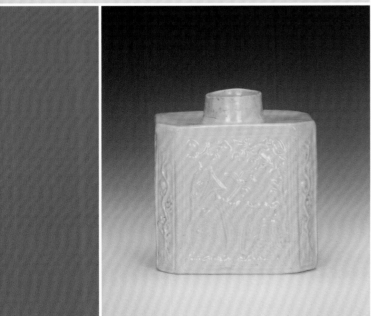

English Staffordshire rectangular flat-shouldered tea caddy with canted corners, c. 1755–60

MATERIALS/DECORATION: Press molded, salt-glazed stoneware with chinoisiere scenes to the front and reverse with vines and flowers to the sides and canted corners. Traces of gilt decoration remain.

MARK: Unmarked

DIMENSIONS: 4¼" H × 3⅝" W × 2⅛" D

MAKER: Unknown

PROVENANCE: Garry Atkins, London. Christie's New York sale of June 14, 2016, sale number 12195, lot 533.

The Trouble with Gilding

Last June I was in London with my great friends Stiles Colwill and Jonathan Gargulio to celebrate George Cooper's sixtieth birthday. I was also having meetings with producers Michael Linnit and Sir Michael Grade, planning the West End revival of *42nd Street*, which I was directing. I got a message from Stiles telling me to get over to Kensington Church Street and see Garry Atkins' display for The Eight Days In June exhibition, as there were two rare tea caddies he thought I might be interested in. My meeting was finished, so I jumped in a cab and went straight to Kensington Church Street to the shop where Garry was having his exhibition, as he no longer keeps a shop of his own. Eight Days In June is an annual event where a group of like-minded specialist dealers, including Simon Spero and Roderick Jellicoe, present a selection of their finest wares in their shops as an alternative to crowded antique shows. When I arrived, Garry showed me the caddies: one early salt glazed stoneware and the other a melon form with green and yellow glazes. While we were chatting Patricia Halfpenny, the well-known ceramics expert, author, and curator emeritus at Winterthur Museum, came into the shop. Garry introduced us and we showed her the salt glazed caddy. As she inspected it, she detected traces of gilt that neither Garry nor I had seen. Pat then told us the most fascinating story about Josiah Wedgwood and the problems he was having with gilt decoration with an outrageous punch line that I loved. Pat kindly sent me the letter, written by Josiah Wedgwood to his brother, from the *Wedgwood Letters*:

> I am very busy every day preparing sprigs, handles, spouts, shapes, making experiments in burning gold &c &c for the service, and from experience I can tell you that sooner I do 'em the more imperfect they will be. I have done a C____ with the new sprigs in green and gold ground, and am very much mortified to find it does not look so well as I expected. The gold ground kills the green, and gives the sprigs a kind of littleness which I must endeavor to get over. Powder gold would do them for me if I knew how to polish it after it is burnt. There is one Jinks who was a gilder in enamel at the Chelsea works, now is at Bow China work; if it would not be too tedious I wish you would buy a cream-color enameled cream ewer and get Jinks to gild all the spaces but the flowers &c and burn the gold in, by which you'll see if he is capable of doing anything for me; and if he does it well he would perhaps tell you how it is polished . . . I believe it is neither a secret or very curious art for women only are employed in it at Chelsea.

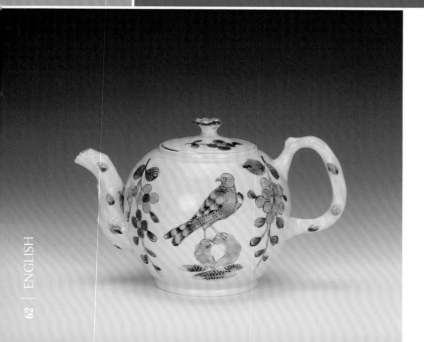

English teapot and cover, c. 1765

MATERIALS/DECORATION: Salt-glazed stoneware decorated with polychrome hawk and blue rock work to the front, three large flower heads to the reverse, and scattered flowers throughout. Flower finial. Very unusual decoration.

MARK: Unmarked

DIMENSIONS: 4¼" H × 7" W × 4¼" D

MAKER: Unknown

PROVENANCE: Michael Grana.

English teapot and cover, c. 1765

MATERIALS/DECORATION: Salt-glazed stoneware decorated in the Chinese famille rose style with a central scroll illustrating a vase and flowers upon a table. Large flower heads to either side. Diaper band with floral panels to the neck and cover, twig handle, finial, and spout.

MARK: Unmarked

DIMENSIONS: 4¼" H × 7¾" W × 4½" D

MAKER: Unknown

PROVENANCE: Peter & Maria Warren Antiques, Wilton, Connecticut.

English teapot and cover, c. 1765

MATERIALS/DECORATION: Salt glaze stoneware decorated in polychrome scenes to the front and reverse. At the front are two musicians: he with a clarinet, she with a lute. On the reverse there are exotic buildings.

MARK: Unmarked

DIMENSIONS: 4¾" H × 8¼" W × 5" D

MAKER: Unknown

PROVENANCE: Peter & Maria Warren Antiques, Wilton, Connecticut.

English conjoined double tea caddy, c. eighteenth century

MATERIALS/DECORATION: Tin-glazed stoneware with a raised decoration of classical Greek figures.

MARK: Unmarked

DIMENSIONS: 5⅜" H × 5½" W × 3⅝" D

MAKER: Unknown

PROVENANCE: Thomaston Place Auction Galleries, Thomaston, Maine.

NOTES: This handwritten note was found inside the caddy: "Towards 1770 excavations at Pompeii and Herculaneum influenced decorations. The brothers Adam and Josiah Wedgwood are associated particularly with this ornamentation. As this piece is not signed (as many of them were not) it is impossible to be sure which potters made it."

English cylindrical tea caddy and cover, c. 1795

MATERIALS/DECORATION: Yellow caneware decorated in the neoclassical style, featuring a central band of figures including satyr and goat, putti, deer, and lion. Crenelated border to the lower third of the body, accented by an interlocking circle border beneath the shoulder, and surrounding the dome cover. Topped by a Weeping Widow finial.

MARK: Impressed "E Mayer"

DIMENSIONS: 5⅝" H × 3" diameter

MAKER: E. Mayer

PROVENANCE: Baltimore Antiques Show.

NOTES: Caneware, a vitreous biscuit or dry body, was first produced in 1790, and was made largely from refined local marls. It was considered an unsatisfactory body by Wedgwood and was not used commercially until about 1776. Caneware was reconstituted again after 1783, and used for tea, coffee, and chocolate services, dejeuner sets, and cabinet pieces. Caneware pieces were decorated by engine turning, encaustic (a mixture of clay and enamel) painting, enameling, and with cast or sprigged relief ornament. The earliest pieces are marked "Wedgwood" in upper and lower case. Caneware was copied by many of Wedgwood's contemporaries, including Mayer and Turner, both of whom produced excellent pieces.

English rectangular shaped tea caddy with canted corners, c. 1800

MATERIALS/DECORATION: Stoneware with black ground, the body molded with raised grape vines and grapes across the surface.

MARK: Unmarked

DIMENSIONS: 4¾" H × 3¼" W × 2¾" D

MAKER: Unknown

English square tea caddy and cover, c. nineteenth century

MATERIALS/DECORATION: Stoneware with molded flower heads and leaves to the front and reverse, and an overall black glaze. Perhaps the decoration was gilded at one time.
MARK: Unmarked
DIMENSIONS: 6" H × 3¼" W × 3¼" D
MAKER: Unknown

English lozenge-shaped tea caddy and cover, c. 1891–1900

MATERIALS/DECORATION: Stoneware with oval panels to the front and reverse, each featuring a large polychrome bird in a simple landscape.
MARK: Copeland late Spode mark.
DIMENSIONS: 5" H × 3¾" W × 2¾" D
MAKER: Spode
PROVENANCE: Bergdorf Goodman, New York.

English lozenge-shaped tea caddy and cover, c. 1910

MATERIALS/DECORATION: Stoneware decorated in printed brick red decoration. At the shoulder is written, "Polly put the kettle on and we'll all have tea."
MARK: Copeland England surrounds Spode's Tower
DIMENSIONS: 5½" H × 4¼" W × 3" D
MAKER: Spode

English lozenge-shaped tea caddy, c. 1910
MATERIALS/DECORATION: Stoneware with blue printed chinoiserie style bucolic landscape. At the shoulder, "Polly put the kettle on and we'll all have tea."
MARK: Copeland England, "Spode's Italian"
DIMENSIONS: 4⅞" H × 4" W × 2⅞" D
MAKER: Spode

English rectangular tea caddy and cover, c. 1913
MATERIALS/DECORATION: Stoneware with fluted corners and Chinese inspired decoration. Figures in blue, yellow, and pink to the front and reverse over a blued "cracked ice" ground. The cover is also decorated in "cracked ice" pattern with a blue band.
MARK: Wm. Adams, England
DIMENSIONS: 5½" H × 4¼" W × 3⅜" W
MAKER: Adams

Thomas Whieldon

Thomas Whieldon was one of the most successful potters of the eighteenth century, and had a lasting influence on the tastes of the time, as well as on the work of the craftsmen that followed him. Whieldon was best known for making Tortoiseshell Ware. He produced this unique type of decoration by applying copper and manganese compounds to earthenware to stain it. Almost immediately after staining the piece would be coated with a clear glaze and fired in a kiln. Whieldon was a shrewd and careful man; to prevent his products being imitated in quality or shape, he buried the wasters (discarded remains of pieces that have been damaged during the manufacturing process). He had many apprentices, including Josiah Spode, Ralph Wood, Robert Garner, William Greatbatch, and Uriah Sutton. From 1754–9, he was in partnership with Josiah Wedgwood. This became a fruitful collaboration, enabling Wedgwood to become a master of the most current pottery techniques. During this time they developed green, yellow, and blue metallic oxide glazes. While in partnership with Whieldon, Wedgwood began his *Experiments Book*, an indelible source on Staffordshire pottery. The introduction states: "This suite of experiments was begun at Fenton Hall, in the Parish of Stoke-on-Trent . . . in my partnership with Mr. Whieldon." When Whieldon retired from the pottery business in 1780, he had amassed a personal fortune of GBP 10,000, which roughly translates into 1.6 million US dollars today. In 1786, he was appointed high sheriff of Staffordshire. Many makers imitated his techniques, and the name "Whieldon-type" is now a generic term describing the style that was developed by Thomas Whieldon.

English cylindrical tea caddy, c. 1775
MATERIALS/DECORATION: Creamware with Whieldon-
   type tortoiseshell design with random green markings.
MARK: Unmarked
DIMENSIONS: 4" H × 3¼" diameter
MAKER: Unknown
PROVENANCE: Sotheby's, New York. The collection
   of Matthew and Elisabeth Sharpe, Conshohocken,
   Pennsylvania; Theodore A. Wiedemann,
   New Hope, Pennsylvania.

Two English square molded tea caddies with dome shoulders, c. 1765
MATERIALS/DECORATION: The first (left) molded
   creamware by William Greatbatch with chinoiserie figures
   in domestic scenes on each side with a pagoda and stylized
   square and circle embellishments to the shoulders. The
   second (right) with a bust-length portrait of Frederick II
   of Prussia, and on the other sides various martial devices,
   including an eagle and a lion with scrolled embellishment
   to the shoulder. Both have been decorated in green,
   brown, and blue Whieldon-type glazes.
MARK: Unmarked
DIMENSIONS: 4¾" H × 2½" W × 2½" D
MAKER: William Greatbatch made the one on the left; the
   maker of the one on the right is unknown
PROVENANCE: Sotheby's, New York. The Greatbatch caddy:
   Sotheby Park Bernet, Inc., New York, property of Mr. Gary
   J. Cheval, April 22, 1981, lot 44. A William Greatbatch
   hexagonal teapot with an identically molded border and
   chinoiserie panels was in the Harriet Carlton Goldweitz
   Collection, sold at Sotheby's, January 20, 2006, lot 143.

English cylindrical tea caddy, c. 1765
MATERIALS/DECORATION: Creamware with brown and
   green Whieldon-type dripped glaze. Three fine incised
   bands circle the lower body.
MARK: Unmarked
DIMENSIONS: 4" H × 3¼" W
MAKER: Unknown
PROVENANCE: Sotheby's, New York. The collection
   of Matthew and Elisabeth Sharpe, Conshohocken,
   Pennsylvania; Theodore A. Wiedmann,
   New Hope, Pennsylvania.

Group of Whieldon type tea wares

English, group of Whieldon-type tea wares. Large globular teapot and cover, cup and saucer with a milk jug, c. 1765–75

MATERIALS/DECORATION: Creamware with applied grape vines encircling the bodies with Whieldon-type brown glaze.

MARK: Unmarked

DIMENSIONS: Teapot is 5¼" H × 8 ¾" W × 5¼" diameter

MAKER: Unknown

PROVENANCE: Teacup and saucer, Jonathan Horne, London; teapot and milk jug purchased in London.

English square tea caddy, c. 1765

MATERIALS/DECORATION: Creamware with molded classical figures in relief on each side. Decorated with green, blue, and yellow Whieldon-type coloration.

MARK: Unmarked

DIMENSIONS: 4¾" H × 2½" W × 2½" D

MAKER: Unknown

PROVENANCE: Patrician Antiques, Los Altos, California, while in San Francisco directing *42nd Street*.

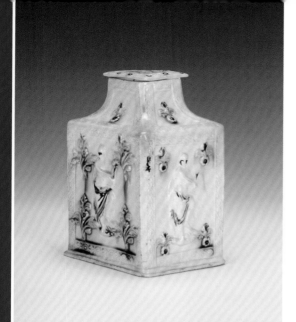

**Large English rectangular tea caddy
with rectangular cap cover, dated 1779**

MATERIALS/DECORATION: Molded creamware with figures
  of neoclassical women playing musical instruments.
  Molded flower heads surround each figure within a florets
  and oval frame. Shoulder similarly decorated. The cover is
  initialed "I.S." and dated 1779. Whieldon-type glazes of
  green, brown, and yellow.

MARK: Unmarked

DIMENSIONS: 6" H × 4¼" W × 3⅜" D

MAKER: Unknown

PROVENANCE: Leo Kaplan, New York.

**English rectangular tea caddy with canted corners,
c. 1775**

MATERIALS/DECORATION: Molded creamware with basket
  weave to the lower body, raised fruit and foliate branches,
  and raised rococo scrolls at each of the canted corners that
  frame each panel. Reeded detail to the shoulder. Lead
  glazed coloration in green, brown, and blue.

MARK: Unmarked

DIMENSIONS: 4¼" H × 3½" W × 2¾" D

MAKER: Attributed to William Greatbatch

PROVENANCE: Purchased in Boston, Massachusetts.

Miniatures were popular with the Dutch.

English assembled miniature Whieldon-type tortoiseshell tea set, c. 1765–85

MATERIALS/DECORATION: Creamware decorated with Whieldon-type tortoiseshell decoration.

MARK: Unmarked

DIMENSIONS: The tea caddy is 2¼" H × 1½" diameter

MAKER: Unknown

PROVENANCE: Tea caddy, sugar bowl, and water kettle from The Antique Flaneur, New York; teapot, cups, and saucers from Leo Kaplan, New York; milk jug from Stockspring Antiques, London.

English globular apple form teapot and cover, c. 1765–75

MATERIALS/DECORATION: Creamware with molded beading at the top of the body and edging of the cover; cover with applied leaves and flower finial. Faux bois handle and spout. Overall glazes in green, brown, and yellow.

MARK: Unmarked

DIMENSIONS: 3¾" H × 5¾" W × 3½" diameter

MAKER: Unknown

PROVENANCE: Purchased on Portobello Road, London, while there with Albert Poland for the memorial service of our great friend, producer Helen Montagu.

English teapot and cover molded in the form of a tree trunk covered in moss, c. 1765–78

MATERIALS/DECORATION: Molded creamware in the form of a tree trunk covered in moss; applied grape vines emanate from the faux bois handle. Colored in Whieldon-type lead glazed colors of green and brown. Cover with a seashell finial.

MARK: Unmarked

DIMENSIONS: 5" H × 8" W × 5" D

MAKER: Unknown

PROVENANCE: Reichner Antiques of Wilmette, Illinois, at the Baltimore Antiques Show.

NOTES: A similar teapot is in the collection of the Dewitt Wallace Museum of Decorative Arts in Williamsburg, Virginia, with the following description: "The remarkable tree stump teapot from the early 1760s is a fully expressive rococo object with nature determining both form and decoration. Its lead glazed earthenware body is slip cast in the form of a tree stump overgrown with moss and fruited grapevines. Its handle and spout appear to be distorted branches growing out of the body. A shell surmounts its asymmetrical cover."

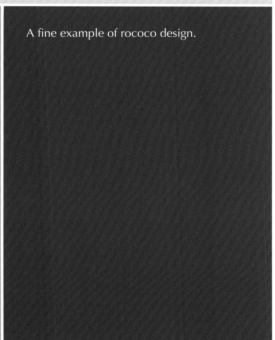

A fine example of rococo design.

English rectangular tea caddy with canted corners and replacement tin cover, c. 1765–75

MATERIALS/DECORATION: Creamware decorated in shades of blue, brown, green, and yellow.

MARK: Unmarked

DIMENSIONS: 4⅞" H × 3⅜" W × 1½" D

MAKER: Unknown

English rectangular tea caddy with sloped-shoulder and canted corners, c. 1770

MATERIALS/DECORATION: Molded creamware with large sprigged flowers and grape vines with a green glaze overall.

MARK: Unmarked

DIMENSIONS: 4½" H × 3" W × 2½" D

MAKER: Unknown

PROVENANCE: Warren Antiques at the New York Ceramic & Glass Fair.

Cauliflower tea wares were very popular.

Cauliflower Ware

The emergence of the rococo style brought with it new excitement in ceramics and a focus on natural forms. The same period produced wares that resembled melons and pineapples marketed to a more selective and affluent customer. These pieces were press-molded in the form of cauliflower. The leaves were painted in a translucent green glaze and the cream florets were coated in a clear glaze. The caddy and waste bowl are attributed to William Greatbatch, who made cauliflower wares from the early 1760s until the end of his career twenty years later. Greatbatch supplied Wedgwood with these, as well as many other wares, and Wedgwood produced his own cauliflower wares from molds supplied by Greatbatch. In his book *British Ceramics 1675–1825*, Brian D. Gallagher writes:

> Cauliflower wares were extremely popular throughout the 1760s and well into the next decade. Wasters have been recovered at Thomas Whieldon's factory site in Fenton . . . in 1766 Wedgwood wrote to Thomas Bentley that he was clearing his warehouse of all colored wares, including the green-glazed ones, as he was "heartily sick of the commodity."

**English Staffordshire cauliflower form tea caddy,
c. 1765**
MATERIALS/DECORATION: Molded creamware in the form
  of a cauliflower.
MARK: Unmarked
DIMENSIONS: 4" H × 3" W × 3" D
MAKER: Attributed to William Greatbatch
PROVENANCE: Jonathan Horne Antiques, London.

**English Staffordshire cauliflower teapot and cover,
c. 1765**
MATERIALS/DECORATION: Molded creamware
  in the form of a cauliflower.
MARK: Unmarked
DIMENSIONS: 6" H × 9" W × 5¼" D
MAKER: Wedgwood
PROVENANCE: Baltimore Antiques Show.

**English Staffordshire slop bowl in the form of a
cauliflower, c. 1765**
MATERIALS/DECORATION: Molded creamware in the form
  of a cauliflower.
MARK: Unmarked
DIMENSIONS: 2½" H × 6½" diameter
MAKER: Attributed to Thomas Whieldon
PROVENANCE: Garry Atkins of London at the New York
  Ceramics & Glass Fair.

English Staffordshire milk jug and cover in the form of a cauliflower, c. 1765

MATERIALS/DECORATION: Molded creamware in the form of a cauliflower.

MARK: Unmarked

DIMENSIONS: 6" H × 4½" W × 3⅕" diameter

MAKER: Attributed to Thomas Whieldon

PROVENANCE: Warren Antiques, Wilton, Connecticut.

English Staffordshire melon ware octagonal tea caddy, c. 1760–65

MATERIALS: Press molded creamware decorated with horizontal rows of rouletted dots, with alternating panels of yellow and green glazes.

MARK: Unmarked

DIMENSIONS: 4¼" H × 2⅞" W × 2⅛" D

MAKER: Possibly Josiah Wedgwood

PROVENANCE: Garry Atkins, London.

NOTES: Based on the brightness of the glazes, it is possible this caddy was made by Josiah Wedgwood, who perfected his green glaze in 1759—in the last year of his partnership with Thomas Whieldon—and his yellow glaze in spring 1760, when he was in business for himself. However, other potters also made these glazes.

Undecorated creamware, c. 1765.

Creamware

As the Staffordshire potters continued their quest to find the elusive arcanum for porcelain, they created a fine white earthenware with a rich yellowish glaze in the 1740s known as creamware. The yellowish glaze came from the use of lead oxide in the glazing process. Josiah Wedgwood, whose extraordinary skills as a ceramic technologist were matched by his talents as a salesman and entrepreneur, made various improvements to creamware and began producing it around 1762 at his factory in Burslem in north Staffordshire (today part of Stoke-On-Trent), the center of Britain's pottery industry. Wedgwood's great commercial success attracted the patronage of Queen Charlotte (1744–1818), wife of King George III. She appointed Wedgwood "Potter To Her Majesty" and he quickly adopted the name "Queen's Ware" for his creamware. His grandest effort was a creamware dinner service of 952 pieces made for Catherine the Great of Russia in 1775, now on view at the Hermitage Museum in St. Petersburg. The "Frog Service" was a fifty-person set intended for dinner and dessert bought by Catherine the Great for her Gothic summer palace built in a frog marsh outside St. Petersburg, hence the inclusion of a frog motif. The service was painted with a total of 1,222 views of British landscapes, country homes, and scenes of industrial progress. One serving dish had a picture of Wedgwood's home, a symbol of his own success as an artist, scientist, and salesman. In the preface to his book *Wedgwood The First Tycoon*, Brian Dolan notes:

> Before sending Catherine's completed service to Russia, Wedgwood displayed it in his London showroom and issued tickets to the public for private viewings. It caused a sensation. Carriages created a roadblock on Greek Street, in Soho, and spectators crowded around to catch a glimpse of the exhibition through the storefront windows as much as to gaze at Wedgwood's aristocratic patrons, who included Queen Charlotte.

By 1790, many English factories (Liverpool, Bristol, and Staffordshire potters among them) had begun extensive creamware production, which supplanted the popularity of salt-glazed stoneware. The success of creamware in domestic and European markets drove many continental stoneware potters to the verge of bankruptcy. Wedgwood was a superstar of the eighteenth century: fashionable, a savvy businessman, and a gifted artist. His genius as a scientist and potter was unparalleled, and his talent as a showman rivaled P. T. Barnum's, as he juggled myriad projects and experiments throughout his life. In 1768, following a long period of suffering with an infection from a childhood disease, he had his leg amputated. Quite by accident he met another one-legged man called Brown, who was a mechanic and engineer. Brown had created an impressive prosthetic leg for himself and had begun a business making wooden legs. Wedgwood engaged Brown to make him a wooden leg. Brian Dolan writes: "Josiah would spare no cost and required a prosthesis carefully crafted to look as much like his previous leg as possible, not only capable of wearing his stocking and shoe but also mechanically jointed so that the foot could move." At the time of his death, Wedgwood's worth was estimated at GBP 600,000, which roughly translates into one hundred million US dollars today.

English rectangular tea caddy with canted corners, c. 1760

MATERIALS/DECORATION: Creamware with naively painted birds on the front and the reverse in iron red and black.

MARK: Unmarked

DIMENSIONS: 4¼" H × 3¼" W × 2½" D

MAKER: Unknown

PROVENANCE: Purchased in Bristol, England.

English cylindrical tea caddy, c. 1765–75

MATERIALS/DECORATION: Creamware with large floral sprays on the front and back in red, greens, and yellow. A fanned pattern in red emanates from the neck.

MARK: Unmarked

DIMENSIONS: 4½" H × 3" diameter

MAKER: Unknown

PROVENANCE: Maria and Peter Warren Antiques at the Village Antique Center, Milbrook, New York.

Creamware teapot.

English teapot and cover, c. 1765–1770

MATERIALS/DECORATION: Creamware with alternating bands of green, yellow, and blue. Ornate double twist handle anchored by well-molded terminals of leaves in green and flowers in yellow. A foliate base to the spout; the domed cover features a large flower head finial sitting in a recessed castellated open neck.

MARK: Unmarked

DIMENSIONS: 5¼" H × 9¼" W × 6¾" diameter

MAKER: Unknown

PROVENANCE: Maria and Peter Warren Antiques at the Village Antiques Center, Milbrook, New York.

NOTES: A similar teapot is in the collection at Winterthur Museum.

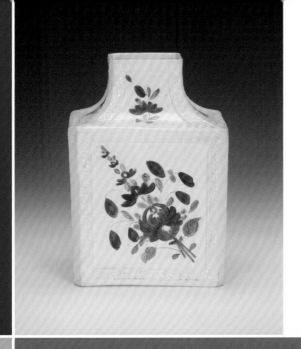

English oversized tea caddy with canted corners, c. 1770
MATERIALS/DECORATION: Creamware painted with flower bouquet in iron red, yellow, and green. Molded egg and flower border.
MARK: Unmarked
DIMENSIONS: 6½" H × 4" W × 3¼" D
MAKER: Unknown
PROVENANCE: Appleby Antiques, Portobello Road, London.
NOTES: Margaret Southwell extensively repaired this caddy.

The Magic of Margaret

Margaret Southwell is a professional ceramic restoration artist. I first encountered her many years ago when a tea caddy I had bought on Portobello Road got broken into a dozen or more pieces on the journey back to the US. I was bemoaning its demise to David Pownall Willis and he told me it could be restored. He offered to take it to Margaret Southwell and see what she could do. When it came back is was like magic. The piece was totally restored without a hint of the damage. How does Margaret do it? In her own words:

Each step is meticulously taken, because if you do not do each step correctly the next step is not correct. It has to be very carefully done, and if you do not do it right, you have to redo it. It is slow, meticulous, patient, observant work, making sure each surface is clean, then gluing it together with epoxy, then filling the crack, and replacing any chip or piece that is missing. I make the new replacement piece out of an epoxy mixture, then smooth it all down with water, or with a certain kind of glass paper (a type of sandpaper that does not scratch the surface) that I get from England. Then you put a glaze over that, smooth that down, then you paint the basic color of the piece—which in your case was creamware—and then you over paint the enamel decoration if needed and then you glaze it.

I asked if she then fired it in a kiln and Margaret explained:

Refiring a piece is dangerous because it can explode, it can get black spots on it, or it can actually burn. So no, it is dangerous and not a risk I take. You can put it in an oven at 200 degrees or put a hair dryer or heat lamp on it to hurry it along. It takes time between each process for things to dry, things to cure, and especially in the filling in of things that you might have to do two or three times. You might have to paint it again if you do not get the right color cream in that light, or it might need more paint, it might need less paint. The whole point is to do as little as possible, but make it look as perfect as possible. And this is hard. Sometimes I put too much paint on and have to take it off. It is not a process that lends itself to being hurried because it is so precise. I rarely work for museums, but people I work for have either donated their collections to museums or the dealers sell to museums. Therefore, I can say I am in the Metropolitan Museum of Art, the High Museum in Atlanta, Kansas City Museum, Columbia Museum, and many private collections. I lived in England. I went over there with my husband, who was doing a master's degree at London University, and I saw an ad in the paper that said "artistic lady wanted." So I answered it and this lady restored antique ceramics. I stayed with her for a year and she kept talking about this place called Sutcliffe's in East Croydon, who were the crème de la crème of restorers for ceramics. So I went out there and worked for them for about a year, then I started working for myself. When I moved back to the United States, I looked through antique magazines at the beautiful adverts of the ceramic dealers and called them up and said "I would like to come and talk to you and show you my work." I began working for Earle Vandekar of Knightsbridge, Leo Kaplan, the Warrens, Millie Manheim, and a number of other dealers, and have been at it for the past thirty years. This is not at all what I expected to do, as I had a BA from New York University in art history and comparative literature, although I started out my life intending to be an opera singer.

English hipp

MATERIALS/
    Leeds-styl
    with smal
    metal ban

MARK: Unma

DIMENSION!

MAKER: Unk

PROVENAN(

English cylindrical tea caddy, c. 1770

MATERIALS/DECORATION: Creamware painted with a large
    central panel of a church with a flowering branch to the
    reverse and a draped swag at the shoulder, all in orange
    and green coloration. The neck has been cut down.
    Probably Dutch decorated.

MARK: Unmarked

DIMENSIONS: 3¾" H × 3" diameter

MAKER: Unknown

English decagon-shaped tea caddy, c. 1770

MATERIALS/DECORATION: Creamware with large
    polychrome bouquets to the front and reverse; scattered
    floral sprays to the sides and shoulder.

MARK: Unmarked

DIMENSIONS: 4" H × 3¼" W × 2½" D

MAKER: Unknown

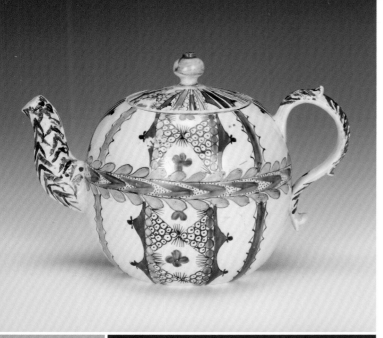

English globular shaped teapot and cover, c. 1770

MATERIALS/DECORATION: Creamware, highly decorated
    in polychrome chintz bands of purple, unusual central
    circular band, and chevrons to the spout and handle.

MARK: Unmarked

DIMENSIONS: 4¾" H × 7¼" W × 4¾" diameter

MAKER: Unknown

English hipped rectangular form tea caddy, c. 1770–80

MATERIALS/DECORATION: Creamware with scattered
    flower sprays to each side and the shoulder. Front panel
    reads, "Green tea".

MARK: Unmarked

DIMENSIONS: 4½" H × 3¼" W × 1¾" D

MAKER: Unknown

PROVENANCE: Garry Atkins of London at the New York
    Ceramics and Glass Fair.

Miniature creamware tea set.

A rare and fine English creamware child's tea set on a circular tray, c. 1770–90

MATERIALS/DECORATION: Undecorated creamware. The set is comprised of a teapot, hot water pitcher, tea caddy, slop bowl, four saucers, four tea bowls, two coffee cups, and a tray.

MARK: Impressed "WEDGWOOD"

DIMENSIONS: Tray 14¼" diameter, teapot 4½" H × 5½" diameter, saucers 3¼" diameter, tea caddy 2½" H × 2" diameter

MAKER: Wedgwood

PROVENANCE: Dean and Mary Rockwell Collection; purchased from Leo Kaplan, New York.

English square tea caddy, dated 1773

MATERIALS/DECORATION: Creamware, with high relief moldings of the goddess Flora on three sides. On the fourth side is a scratch brown inscription with flowers reading, "Joan Tozer, 1773."

MARK: Unmarked

DIMENSIONS: 6" H × 4½" W × 4½" D

MAKER: Bovey Tracey

PROVENANCE: Dallas Auction Gallery, Dallas, Texas; similar caddy sold at Sotheby's, New York, June 20, 2000; similar caddy sold at Sotheby's, New York, February 22, 1988, lot 553.

NOTES: The Bovey Tracey Pottery Company was established in the mid-eighteenth century in the small town Bovey Tracy, Devon. Clay from the River Bovey provided material for a pottery industry that profited from being a good distance (175 miles) from the potteries in Stoke On Trent, allowing the company to thrive with a strong local market. The factory produced everyday wares in salt-glaze and creamware. Attempts to manufacture porcelain failed. A similar caddy was exhibited in the 2002 Tea, Trade And Tea Cannisters exhibition at Stockspring Antiques, London, appearing in the catalog of that event (number 7).

English beehive-shaped tea caddy, c. 1775

MATERIALS/DECORATION: Creamware decorated with puce scattered flowers and insects.

MARK: Unmarked

DIMENSIONS: 4½" H × 4" diameter

MAKER: Unknown

PROVENANCE: Bob Moores, London.

English hipped rectangular tea caddy and cover, c. 1775

MATERIALS/DECORATION: Molded creamware with raised laurel leaves with putti figures to the front and reverse, and pendant swags hanging from ribbons at the shoulder. There is a large sunflower medallion to either side of the upper shoulder.

MARK: "WEDGWOOD"

DIMENSIONS: 5" H × 2¾" W × 2" D

MAKER: Wedgwood

PROVENANCE: Stockspring Antiques, London.

English cylindrical tea caddy and cover, c. 1780

MATERIALS/DECORATION: Creamware painted with scattered floral and foliate to the body and cover with floral swags hanging from the shoulder. There are pink bands at the shoulder.

MARK: Unmarked

DIMENSIONS: 5" H × 3½" diameter

MAKER: Unknown

PROVENANCE: David Pownall Willis, Plainfield, New Jersey.

English rectangular sloped-shoulder tea caddy, c. 1780
MATERIALS/DECORATION: Undecorated creamware.
MARK: Unmarked
DIMENSIONS: 4¾" H × 3" W × 1¾" W
MAKER: Unknown

English cylindrical tea caddy with rounded shoulder, c. 1780
MATERIALS/DECORATION: Creamware with polychrome Leeds-type decoration with floral bouquets to the front and back and scattered flowers to the shoulders.
MARK: Unmarked
DIMENSIONS: 3½" H × 3⅛" diameter
MAKER: Unknown
PROVENANCE: Purchased in England; label on the bottom reads "Donald Towner Collection". Mr. Towner wrote the 1978 book *Creamware*, published by Faber and Faber.

English cylindrical tea caddy with rounded shoulder, c. 1780
MATERIALS/DECORATION: Creamware with a large panel to the front featuring the anointing of Saul by Samuel: "1 Samuel 10:1" appears beneath the image. There are simple floral and foliate vines upon the sides and reverse.
MARK: Unmarked
DIMENSIONS: 4" H × 3¼" diameter
MAKER: Unknown
PROVENANCE: Art and Cathy Green, Early Glass And Ceramics of Newton Center, Massachusetts, at the Baltimore Antiques Show.
NOTE: This was probably Dutch decorated.

English hipped rectangular tea caddy, c. 1780

MATERIALS/DECORATION: Creamware with a printed scene of a shepherd and his sheep. On the reverse is the tea party design. A strong mold line to either side.

MARK: Unmarked

DIMENSIONS: 4" H × 3¼" W × 2" D

MAKER: Unknown

PROVENANCE: Semley Auctioneers, Shaftesbury, England.

A pair of English cylindrical tea caddies, c. 1780

MATERIALS/DECORATION: Creamware with polychrome painted floral bouquets to the front and back with small floral swags to the shoulders.

MARK: Unmarked

DIMENSIONS: 3½" H × 3⅛" diameter

MAKER: Unknown

PROVENANCE: Bob Moores, London.

English hipped rectangular tea caddy with canted corners, circa c. 1780

MATERIALS/DECORATION: Creamware with a printed scene of a shepherd and his sheep in rare brown coloration. On the reverse is the tea party design, also in brown. Strong mold line to both sides.

MARK: Unmarked

DIMENSIONS: 4" H × 2¾" W × 2½" D

MAKER: Unknown

English cylindrical tea caddy and cover, c. 1780

MATERIALS/DECORATION: Creamware printed in black with birds on a fence to one side and a woman walking with two children on the reverse. There is a painted border to the shoulder, cover, and finial.

MARK: Unmarked

DIMENSIONS: 5¼" H × 3¼" diameter

MAKER: Unknown

PROVENANCE: David Pownall Willis, Plainfield, New Jersey.

English cylindrical tea caddy, c. 1780

MATERIALS/DECORATION: Creamware decorated with the Pratt colors depicting a scrolling vine and leaf that circles the body with a yellow band to the base, shoulder, and neck.

MARK: Small blue "x" tally mark

DIMENSIONS: 4" H × 3¹⁄₁₆" diameter

MAKER: Unknown

NOTES: Prattware was developed by Felix Pratt, and was made by various potters between 1780 and 1840. The colors were applied under the glaze and were limited to the oxide colors that could withstand the heat necessary to fuse the glaze: blue, yellow, orange, green, brown, and black. Occasionally a dark raspberry color was introduced. The lead glaze was often slightly tinted with blue.

English cylindrical tea caddy with later silver-colored cover, c. 1785

MATERIALS/DECORATION: Creamware with mottled salmon ground with outside decorated panels. Circular panels to the front and back are naively painted with a galloping horse, and two leaf-shaped panels to either side with flower sprays.

MARK: Unmarked

DIMENSIONS: 4⅝" H × 3⅜" diameter

MAKER: Unknown

PROVENANCE: Purchased in Newport, New Hampshire.

English cylindrical tea caddy, c. 1785–90

MATERIALS/DECORATION: Creamware with blue and white painted chinoiserie scenes with pagodas, plants, and zigzag fence pattern decoration.

MARK: Unmarked

DIMENSIONS: 4" H × 3⅛" diameter

MAKER: Unknown

PROVENANCE: Purchased from the collection of H. C. Van Vliet, Amsterdam.

English flask form tea caddy, c. 1785–1800

MATERIALS/DECORATION: Creamware with molded putti figures carrying grapes upon an incised dotted ground. Decorated with the Pratt colors green, yellow and blue; a molded leaf with feathered edge to each side.

MARK: Unmarked

DIMENSIONS: 4" H × 2⅝" W × 2¼" D

MAKER: Unknown

PROVENANCE: Gerald Clark Antiques of Edgeware at the Winter Art & Antiques Fair, Olympia, London.

English cylindrical tea caddy, c. 1785
MATERIALS/DECORATION: Creamware with a polychrome decoration of red rose and flower bouquet; shoulders are similarly decorated.
MARK: Unmarked
DIMENSIONS: 3½" H × 2½" diameter
MAKER: Unknown

English creamware decagonal tea caddy and cover, c. 1785
MATERIALS/DECORATION: Creamware printed with a shepherd and his animals beneath a tree to the front, and to the reverse a couple seated at a table beneath a tree having tea. Cover is decorated with rosettes; all decoration in rust-red coloration.
MARK: Unmarked
DIMENSIONS: 4¼" H × 3" W × 4¾" D
MAKER: Unknown

English octagonal tea caddy, c. 1785
MATERIALS/DECORATION: Creamware with puce decoration of flowers to the front and reverse. Flowerets on the shoulder.
MARK: Unmarked
DIMENSIONS: 4⅞" H × 4½" W × 3" D
MAKER: Unknown
PROVENANCE: Maria & Peter Warren Antiques of Wilton, Connecticut, at Northeast Auctions, Portsmouth, New Hampshire.

English milk jug, c. 1785
MATERIALS/DECORATION: Creamware decorated with a puce central flower bouquet with scattered leaves to the body; the double loop handle has polychrome green and pink terminals.
MARK: Unmarked
DIMENSIONS: 5¼" H × 4½" W
MAKER: Unmarked
PROVENANCE: Maria & Peter Warren Antiques of Wilton, Connecticut, at Northeast Auctions, Portsmouth, New Hampshire.

English globular teapot and cover, c. 1785

MATERIALS/DECORATION: Creamware decorated with a
    puce central flower bouquet with leaves scattered to the
    corners to the front and reverse; the reeded double loop
    handle has polychrome green and pink terminals.
MARK: Unmarked
DIMENSIONS: 5" H × 8¼" W × 4¾" diameter
MAKER: Unknown
PROVENANCE: Maria & Peter Warren Antiques of Wilton,
    Connecticut, at Northeast Auctions, Portsmouth,
    New Hampshire.

English cylindrical rounded shoulder tea caddy, c. 1785

MATERIALS/DECORATION: Creamware decorated with leaf
    garland and pendants hanging from a pink band at the
    shoulder. Flower sprays to the shoulder.
MARK: Unmarked
DIMENSIONS: 3¼" H × 3¾" diameter
MAKER: Unknown
PROVENANCE: Purchased from the collection of H. C. Van
    Vliet, Amsterdam, while there directing *42nd Street*.

English hipped rectangular tea caddy and cover, c. 1785

MATERIALS/DECORATION: Creamware decorated with
    puce flower sprays to the front and reverse. There are floral
    sprigs to the sides, top of the shoulder, and cover.
MARK: Unmarked
DIMENSIONS: 6" H × 3⅓" W × 2½" W
MAKER: Unknown
PROVENANCE: Maria & Peter Warren Antiques
    at the Village Antiques Center in Milbrook, New York.

English creamware engine turned cylindrical tea caddy, c. 1790

MATERIALS/DECORATION: Undecorated creamware with
    five bands surrounding the body, a beaded border to the
    base, and top.
MARK: Unmarked
DIMENSIONS: 4" H × 2⅞" diameter
MAKER: Unknown
PROVENANCE: Purchased in London.

English cylindrical sloped-shoulder tea caddy and cover, milk jug, and slop bowl, c. 1790

MATERIALS/DECORATION: Creamware decorated in green enamel laurel swags hanging from the sloped shoulder; scattered flowers and leaf boughs to the shoulder and cover.

MARK: Unmarked

DIMENSIONS: The tea caddy is 5¾" H × 3¼" diameter

MAKER: Unknown

PROVENANCE: Caddy from Hanes and Ruskin Antiques, Old Lyme, Connecticut. Slop bowl and jug purchased in Amsterdam.

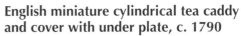

English miniature cylindrical tea caddy and cover with under plate, c. 1790

MATERIALS/DECORATION: Creamware with painted green feathered edge at the shoulder, base of the cover, and around the edge of the under plate.

MARK: Unmarked

DIMENSIONS: Tea caddy: 3½" H × 2" diameter; plate; 4½" diameter

MAKER: Unknown

NOTES: Similar tea caddy in figure #1 of *English Toy China* by Doris Anderson Lechler.

English cylindrical tea caddy, c. 1790

MATERIALS/DECORATION: Creamware with alternating bands of green against a plain reeded body.

MARK: Unmarked

DIMENSIONS: 3¼" H × 3½" diameter

MAKER: Unknown

PROVENANCE: Maria & Peter Warren Antiques at the Village Antique Center, Milbrook, New York.

English cylindrical tea caddy, c. 1790–1800

MATERIALS/DECORATION: Creamware with hand painted underglaze blue flower and vine decoration on the reeded body and shoulder.

MARK: Unmarked

DIMENSIONS: 4½" H × 4" diameter

MAKER: Unknown

PROVENANCE: Maria & Peter Warren Antiques at the New York Ceramics Fair.

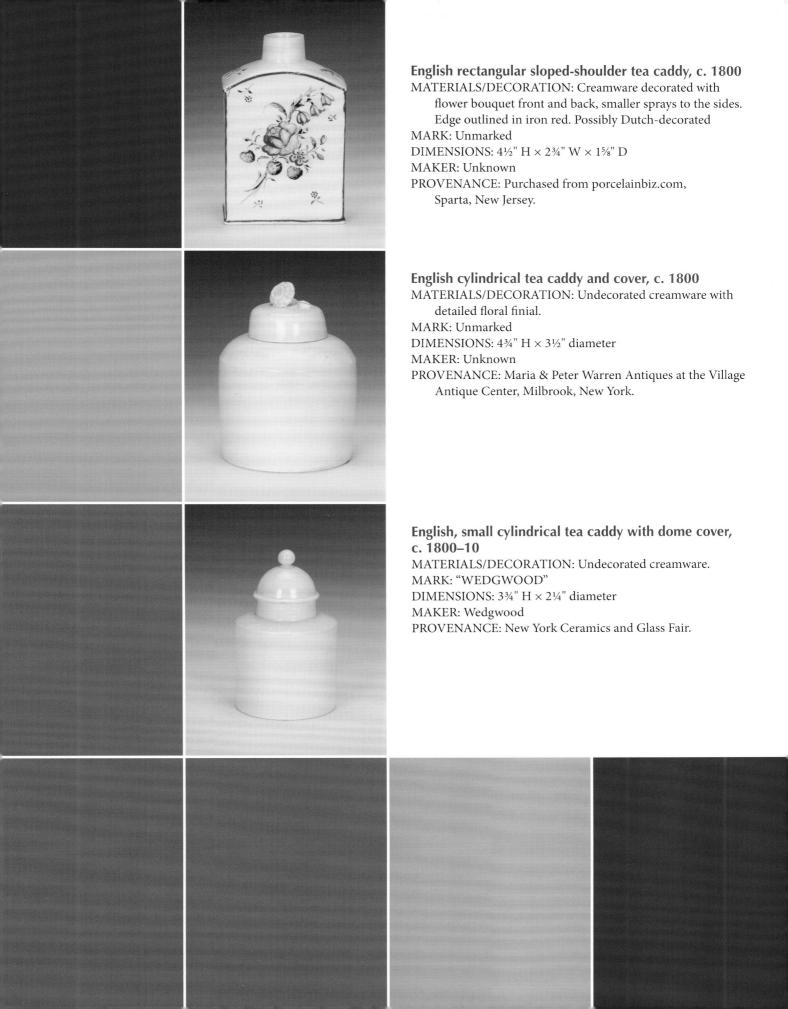

English rectangular sloped-shoulder tea caddy, c. 1800

MATERIALS/DECORATION: Creamware decorated with
 flower bouquet front and back, smaller sprays to the sides.
 Edge outlined in iron red. Possibly Dutch-decorated

MARK: Unmarked

DIMENSIONS: 4½" H × 2¾" W × 1⅝" D

MAKER: Unknown

PROVENANCE: Purchased from porcelainbiz.com,
 Sparta, New Jersey.

English cylindrical tea caddy and cover, c. 1800

MATERIALS/DECORATION: Undecorated creamware with
 detailed floral finial.

MARK: Unmarked

DIMENSIONS: 4¾" H × 3½" diameter

MAKER: Unknown

PROVENANCE: Maria & Peter Warren Antiques at the Village
 Antique Center, Milbrook, New York.

English, small cylindrical tea caddy with dome cover, c. 1800–10

MATERIALS/DECORATION: Undecorated creamware.

MARK: "WEDGWOOD"

DIMENSIONS: 3¾" H × 2¼" diameter

MAKER: Wedgwood

PROVENANCE: New York Ceramics and Glass Fair.

The Leeds Revival Ceramics

I purchased a pair of undecorated creamware tea caddies, believing they were Leeds, dating to 1770 or '80. When Paul Vandekar and Deidre Healy examined these caddies, they believed that they were not from the late eighteenth or nineteenth century, but that they were early twentieth century caddies using the earlier molds. Paul confirmed his suspicions with Alan Kaplan of Leo Kaplan Ltd. and explained it thusly:

There is an interesting group of creamware objects, often impressed Leeds Pottery, which differ somewhat from traditional eighteenth and early nineteenth century creamware. This story is well covered by John D. Griffin's research revealed in his important book, *The Leeds Pottery, 1770–1881, Volume II* (pp 603–624). Several members of the Senior family and James Morton made the pieces. These later pieces are sometimes referred to as being manufactured by a man called W. W. Slee. This erroneous information derives from a 1913 catalog in which Slee claimed that he revived the manufacture of Leeds Pottery in 1888, employing workmen and using original molds. None of that was true. Slee, in fact, sold creamware that was manufactured by others. In the late nineteenth and early twentieth century, typical eighteenth century Leeds Pottery creamware was produced by members of the Senior family, principally James "Wraith" Senior, who worked over time with his sons, George William and James Jr., and his brother-in-law, potter John Thomas Morton (1875–1956). Morton was an apprentice to James Senior circa 1888–1895, and returned to work with the Seniors from 1907 to circa 1913, when he left to establish his own pottery.

According to John Griffin, it is virtually impossible to distinguish between pieces made by Morton when potting on his own and those produced by the Senior brothers. The Senior reproductions, sometimes using original molds, often bear that same original impressed "LEEDS POTTERY" mark as used by the Hartley, Green, and Co. Leeds factory. The Seniors' body is often more thickly potted than the original, and the glaze is often grayer and more thickly applied, which then pooled (often with a green tone) with a very distinct crackled glaze. However, their wares can also be of such high quality that they can be mistaken for the work of earlier factories. While the revival creamware was the Seniors' main business, they did develop many forms with pierced designs that were original to them. George William Senior, in an interview in 1967, said that large consignments of pottery were made to the United States and France, and pieces made for the United States were specially "crazed" to conform to customers' taste. These revival creamwares helped meet the demand in America for colonial revival ceramics in the same way factories such as those in Dresden, Vienna, and Samson in Paris did for porcelain. Great homes for the newly wealthy were being built from Newport to New York and all across the United States, and thus the demand for such pieces was high. These revival pieces were often used to decorate those great houses.

Pair of English Leeds (Slee) hipped rectangular tea caddies with canted corners and domed covers, c. 1900

MATERIALS/DECORATION: Undecorated creamware
MARK: Unmarked
DIMENSIONS: 5½" H × 3¹⁄₁₆" W × 2⅜" D
MAKER: Unmarked
PROVENANCE: Maria & Peter Warren Antiques, Wilton, Connecticut.

Pearlware

Creamware continued to be popular throughout the nineteenth century and beyond. Salt-glazed stoneware fell out of fashion around 1800, and there was little production of it after that. By 1779, Wedgwood began using a white to bluish-white glaze he called "pearl white" which became known as "pearl ware." By adding a bit of cobalt to the glaze, the blue made the creamware appear brighter and whiter. It was an immediate success, and was popular for nearly a century. Other Staffordshire potters had been using this glaze from as early as 1775, calling it "China glaze." Interestingly, one of the most common earthenwares found on American archaeological sites from the late eighteenth century and early nineteenth century is pearlware, indicating just how many British ceramics Americans imported during this period.

English hipped rectangular tea caddy with canted corners and cover, c. 1780–1800

MATERIALS/DECORATION: Molded pearlware decorated in the Pratt colors featuring the Muses in relief to the front and reverse: one gathering flowers in a scarf and the second holding a pendant garland. To the sides, a chinoiserie pagoda and herringbone border within the canted corners. Pagoda-shaped cover.

MARK: Unmarked

DIMENSIONS: 6½" H × 3¾" W × 2¼" D

MAKER: Unknown

PROVENANCE: Gerald Clark Antiques at the Olympia Winter Antiques Show, London.

English cylindrical tea caddy, c. 1780

MATERIALS/DECORATION: Pearlware with underglaze blue and white decoration featuring chinoiserie landscape with two birds flying overhead on the front; on the reverse chinoiserie fence runs through a meadow with rocks and flowers. A fine double blue band runs around the slightly sloped shoulder.

MARK: Unmarked

DIMENSIONS: 4" H × 3¼" diameter

MAKER: Unknown

English cylindrical tea caddy, c. 1780

MATERIALS/DECORATION: Pearlware with sponged green leaves framing a polychrome peafowl on a branch.

MARK: Unmarked

DIMENSIONS: 4" H × 3¼" diameter

MAKER: Unknown

PROVENANCE: Maria & Peter Warren Antiques of Wilton, Connecticut, at the Village Antiques Center, Milbrook, New York.

NOTES: Similar caddy exhibited in the 2002 Tea, Trade And Tea Cannisters exhibition at Stockspring Antiques, London, appearing in the catalog of that event (number 155).

English cylindrical tea caddy and cover, c. 1780

MATERIALS/DECORATION: Pearlware with printed underglaze blue featuring Chinese figures and a pagoda with an ornate scale ground band with rococo designs to the shoulder and edge of the cover. The finial is similarly decorated.

MARK: Unmarked

DIMENSIONS: 6⅛" H × 3½" diameter

MAKER: Unknown

PROVENANCE: New York Pier Show.

English hipped rectangular tea caddy with canted corners, c. 1780

MATERIALS/DECORATION: Pearlware with pink polychrome roses front and back with scattered leaves to the sides and shoulder. The upper shoulder is decorated with an outer band in small iron red pendants.

MARK: Unmarked

DIMENSIONS: 4⅝" H × 3½" W × 2¼" D

MAKER: Unknown

PROVENANCE: Two Birds Antiques of Chicago, at the Baltimore Antiques Show.

English miniature cylindrical tea caddy, c. 1780–90

MATERIALS/DECORATION: Pearlware with a deep underglaze blue chinoiserie decoration of buildings and stylized trees in the landscape around the body.

MARK: Unmarked

DIMENSIONS: 2½" H × 2" diameter

MAKER: Unknown

PROVENANCE: Purchased in London.

English cylindrical tea caddy and cover, c. 1780–1800

MATERIALS/DECORATION: Pearlware with a blue and white printed design featuring large flower heads and leaves in the chinoiserie style. Later silver collar and cover.

MARK: Unmarked

DIMENSIONS: 5⁹⁄₁₆" H × 3½" diameter

MAKER: Unknown

PROVENANCE: Purchased from the collection of H. C. Van Vliet, Amsterdam.

English cylindrical tea caddy and cover, c. 1780–1800

MATERIALS/DECORATION: Batavia ware-inspired pearlware with a brown slip ground with three blue and white floral bouquets, each within a shaped panel. Blue and white decoration at the shoulder and base of the cover.

MARK: Unmarked

DIMENSIONS: 5¼" H × 3½" diameter

MAKER: Unknown

PROVENANCE: Purchased from the collection of H. C. Van Vliet, Amsterdam.

NOTES: Batavia ware is named for the city of Batavia in Indonesia (now Jakarta), one of the main trading posts of the Dutch East India Company. This type of brown slip decoration remained popular in Holland throughout the eighteenth century.

English hipped rectangular tea caddy with dome cover, c. 1780–1800

MATERIALS/DECORATION: Pearlware with a hand painted blue mountainous landscape to the body and stylized botanicals to the shoulder and cover.

MARK: Unmarked

DIMENSIONS: 5¼" H × 2¾" W × 2" D

MAKER: Unknown

PROVENANCE: New York Ceramics And Glass Fair.

English cylindrical tea caddy, c. 1780–1800

MATERIALS/DECORATION: Pearlware with underglaze a blue and white printed "fence and flowers" pattern in the chinoiserie style on the front, and on the reverse two birds fly over a landscape. Around the shoulder there is a double blue band.

MARK: Unmarked

DIMENSIONS: 4" H × 3" diameter

MAKER: Unknown

English cylindrical tea caddy and cover, c. 1780–1800

MATERIALS/DECORATION: Pearlware with underglaze blue and white printed "fence and flowers" pattern in the chinoiserie style on the front; on the reverse two birds fly over a landscape. There is a double blue band at the base of the neck and around the bottom of the cover, which has a flower finial. This is a copy of a Worcester design.

MARK: Faux full crescent Worcester mark

DIMENSIONS: 5¼" H × 3" diameter

MAKER: Unknown

PROVENANCE: New York Pier Show.

English cylindrical tea caddy with replacement metal cover, c. 1785

MATERIALS/DECORATION: Pearlware with overglaze polychrome decoration of flowers to the body and shoulder. On the front, within a wreath of flowers, is written "Bohea Tea" in black.

MARK: Unmarked

DIMENSIONS: 4" H × 3¼" diameter

MAKER: Unknown, possibly William Greatbatch

PROVENANCE: Purchased on Portobello Road, London.

English cylindrical tea caddy, c. 1785–90

MATERIALS/DECORATION: Pearlware with transfer printed floral motif.

MARK: Unmarked

DIMENSIONS: 3¾" H × 3" diameter

MAKER: Unknown

PROVENANCE: Purchased from the collection of H. C. Van Vliet, Amsterdam.

English fluted baluster shape with drop in pagoda style cover, c. 1790–1800

MATERIALS/DECORATION: Pearlware decorated in pale green, brown, pink, and blue enamels with floral swags. Green bands to the neck, rim, and finial; brown band at the shoulder. The fluted lid is decorated with floral swags and a rounded knob.

MARK: Unmarked

DIMENSIONS: 5¼" H × 3¼" diameter

MAKER: Unknown, probably Staffordshire

NOTES: Similar caddy exhibited in the 2002 Tea, Trade And Tea Cannisters exhibition at Stockspring Antiques, London, appearing in the catalog of that event (number 178).

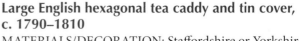

Large English hexagonal tea caddy and tin cover, c. 1790–1810

MATERIALS/DECORATION: Staffordshire or Yorkshire molded pearlware decorated in the "Chinese Pagodas" pattern. The panels are painted in underglaze blue with three pagodas flanked by flowering plants within molded foliate borders. At the shoulder there is a border of leaf tips heightened in underglaze green.

MARK: Unmarked

DIMENSIONS: 5⅛" H × 4¾" W × 3⅝" D

MAKER: Unknown

PROVENANCE: Northeast Auctions, Portsmouth, New Hampshire

NOTES: For additional information regarding an identical caddy and similar wares see George L. Miller and Robert Hunter's article in *Ceramics In America* entitled "How Creamware Got The Blues: The Origins Of China Glaze And Pearlware," (pp 135–161).

English cylindrical tea caddy, c. 1790

MATERIALS/DECORATION: Pearlware with a repeating floral design of scattered flower heads to the body and shoulder.

MARK: Painted "v"

DIMENSIONS: 4" H × 3¼" diameter

MAKER: Unknown

English cylindrical tea caddy, c. 1790

MATERIALS/DECORATION: Pearlware with an engine-turned band in black and white at the shoulder upon a blue ground.

MARK: Unmarked

DIMENSIONS: 4¼" H × 3" diameter

MAKER: Unknown

PROVENANCE: The collection of H. C. Van Vliet, Amsterdam.

English hipped rectangular tea caddy, c. 1790
MATERIALS/DECORATION: Pearlware decorated in blue
and white; a festooned pendant swag "hangs" from the
lower edge of the shoulder.
MARK: Unmarked
DIMENSIONS: 4½" H × 3⅝" W × 2¼" D
MAKER: Unknown
PROVENANCE: Purchased from Rose Victoria Antiques,
Orange County, California.

English covered round container, c. 1790
MATERIALS/DECORATION: Pearlware with a deep blue
feathered edge molded and painted underglaze. Cover
with a molded dark blue band.
MARK: Unmarked
DIMENSIONS: 4" H × 2⅛" diameter
MAKER: Unknown

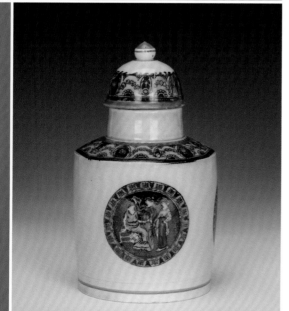

**English cylindrical tea caddy with domed cover,
c. 1790–1800**
MATERIALS/DECORATION: Pearlware with a printed
decoration featuring three neoclassical panels of the
Muses within green wreath borders. Ornate green printed
band at the shoulder and lower half of the cover with
ochre bands at the base, base of the neck, bottom of the
cover, and finial.
MARK: Unmarked
DIMENSIONS: 6¼" H × 3¼" diameter
MAKER: Unknown
PROVENANCE: Seekers Antiques of Columbus, Ohio,
at the Baltimore Antiques Show.

English modified lozenge-shaped tea caddy with hipped shoulders to all four convex sides, c. 1790–1800

MATERIALS/DECORATION: Molded Pearlware with reeded columns to the corners. There is blue and yellow underglaze decoration featuring a large yellow flower with blue sprays behind. Blue floral sprays and a feathered edge to the shoulder.

MARK: Unmarked

DIMENSIONS: 4½" H × 3¾" W × 3" D

MAKER: Unknown

PROVENANCE: Suzanne Fischer Antiques, Chestertown, Maryland.

NOTES: Similar caddy exhibited in the 2002 Tea, Trade And Tea Cannisters exhibition at Stockspring Antiques, London, appearing in the catalog of that event (number 118).

English teapot and cover, c. 1790

MATERIALS/DECORATION: Pearlware featuring large panels to the front and reverse, both signed "J. Ainsley at Lane End." Decorated with pink bands to the upper neck and rim of the cover; to the front a central roundel with a gentleman beneath a compass and the legend, "Keep Within compass and you shall be sure to avoid many dangers which others endure." On the reverse there is a roundel with a lady and similar text. The images and writing reveal a morality play. Images on the left of each roundel represent a life of virtue, those on the right, one of debauchery. There is a pink painted flower to the round finial and dots to the top of the handle.

MARK: None to the body, although the images are signed

DIMENSIONS: 5¼" H × 9" W × 5½" diameter

MAKER: Lane End

PROVENANCE: Maria & Peter Warren Antiques, Wilton, Connecticut.

NOTES: A similar teapot appears in *The British Museum Catalogue Of English Pottery* (p 263). A note found inside the teapot reads: "there are only 6 of these signed teapots known to exist. It represents a rare moment of ceramic and social history."

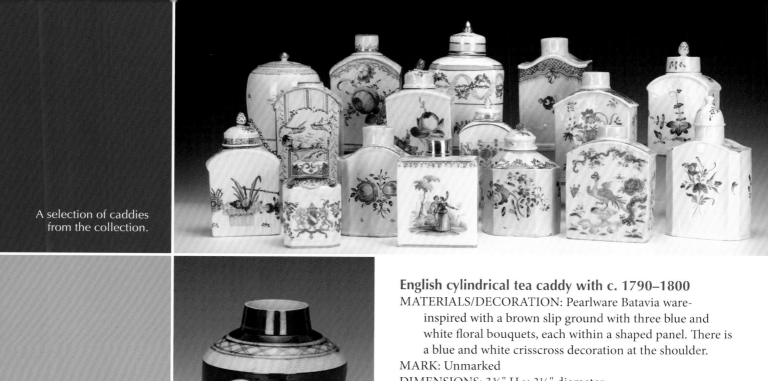

A selection of caddies from the collection.

English cylindrical tea caddy with c. 1790–1800

MATERIALS/DECORATION: Pearlware Batavia ware-inspired with a brown slip ground with three blue and white floral bouquets, each within a shaped panel. There is a blue and white crisscross decoration at the shoulder.

MARK: Unmarked

DIMENSIONS: 3¾" H × 3½" diameter

MAKER: Unknown

PROVENANCE: The Collection of H. C. Van Vliet, Amsterdam, purchased while in Holland casting the Dutch production of *42nd Street*.

NOTES: Possibly made for the Dutch market.

English hipped rectangular sloped-shoulder tea caddy, c. 1790–1810

MATERIALS/DECORATION: Molded pearlware with Macaroni figures and decorated in the Pratt colors.

MARK: Unmarked

DIMENSIONS: 4⅞" H × 3½" W × 2 ¼" D

PROVENANCE: Harmic-Little Antiques, Middletown, Delaware.

NOTES: The term "Macaroni" probably comes from the Italian word *maccherone*, which means a fool. Macaroni in eighteenth century England refers to a group of Britons who spoke and dressed so pretentiously that they inspired great mockery. These young men wore rouged lips, powdered wigs, lace collars and cuffs, extravagant jewelry, and polished nails. It also refers to the Macaroni Club, a trendy dining club that featured foreign foods such as macaroni (*see top p 100*).

Etching of macaronis. *Author's collection*

English cylindrical tea caddy, c. 1800

MATERIALS/DECORATION: Pearlware with a printed black scene of a shepherd, dog, and sheep in a landscape to the front and a couple being served tea on the reverse. A black band encircles the shoulder.

MARK: Unmarked

DIMENSIONS: 4¼" H × 3¹⁄₁₆" diameter

MAKER: Unknown

PROVENANCE: Purchased on Portobello Road, London.

English decagonal tea caddy and cover, c. 1810

MATERIALS/DECORATION: Pearlware with enameled bouquets to the front and back; smaller bouquets to the sides. Faux diaper and floral border to the shoulder. Cover with small flower buds and grape finial.

MARK: Unmarked

DIMENSIONS: 4¾" H × 3¾" W × 2⅜" diameter

MAKER: Unknown

PROVENANCE: Purchased from the Gould estate sale at Russum's Antiques in Crumpton, Maryland.

Pair of English cylindrical tea caddies, c. 1810–20

MATERIALS/DECORATION: Pearlware, each with three
 black-and-white printed scenes of the Muses within a
 wreath border; a printed ornate border fills the shoulder.
MARK: Unmarked
DIMENSIONS: 4¼" H × 3½" diameter
MAKER: Unknown

English cylindrical tea caddy, c. 1820

MATERIALS/DECORATION: Pearlware with a printed black
 chinoisiere pagoda and river panels to the front and
 reverse; an ornate printed diaper to the shoulder.
MARK: Unmarked
DIMENSIONS: 4" H × 3¾" diameter
MAKER: Unknown

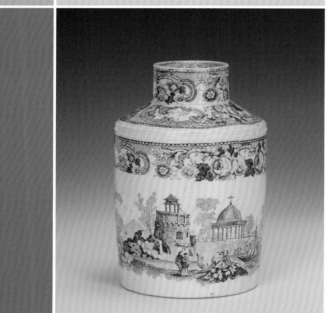

English cylindrical tea caddy c. 1830

MATERIALS/DECORATION: Pearlware decorated with
 a printed country life scene in mulberry with a lappet
 border. Shoulder and neck are covered in a wide
 lappet border.
MARK: Unmarked
DIMENSIONS: 5" H × 3¼" diameter
MAKER: Unknown
PROVENANCE: Purchased from Rose Victoria Antiques,
 Orange County, California.

English lozenge-shaped tea caddy and domed cover, c. 1850

MATERIALS/DECORATION: Pearlware decorated with florets and bands of silver lustre and iron red to the upper body and cover.

MARK: In silver lustre: "A5641" with a "v" beneath

DIMENSIONS: 5¼" H × 3¾" W × 2¾" D

MAKER: Possibly Wedgwood

PROVENANCE: Mimi's Antiques, Columbia, Maryland.

English rectangular tea caddy with canted corners and associated black metal cover, c. 1860

MATERIALS/DECORATION: Pearlware with a blue and white chinoiserie landscape scene to the front and back, embellished network diaper border to the shoulder.

MARK: Unmarked

DIMENSIONS: 5" H × 4" W × 3¼" D

MAKER: Unknown

PROVENANCE: Purchased in England.

English, large blue and white flared square-shaped tea caddy and cover, twentieth century reproduction

MATERIALS/DECORATION: Pearlware with printed underglaze blue decoration of a landscape with figures on a bridge, trees, and pagodas.

MARK: "RINGTONS LIMITED/TEA MERCHANTS/ NEWCASTLE UPON TYNE"

DIMENSIONS: 7¾" H × 4½" W × 4½" D

MAKER: Unknown

English, large blue and white flared square-shaped tea caddy, twentieth century reproduction

MATERIALS/DECORATION: Pearlware printed with an underglaze blue chinoiserie pagoda and river scene circling the body. Ornate Chinese-inspired border at the base, shoulder, and cover.

MARK: "RINGTONS LIMITED/TEA MERCHANTS/ NEWCASTLE UPON TYNE"

DIMENSIONS: 8" H × 5½" W × 4½" D

MAKER: Unknown

Chapter 5
ENGLISH PORCELAIN

It was not until the 1760s—half a century after the Germans were creating true porcelain—that William Cookworthy made the first true hard-paste porcelain in Britain. He was a Quaker minister, pharmacist, and inventor who discovered deposits of kaolin and pentuntse—a variety of feldspar also known as "china stone"—at St. Austell in Cornwall. Having finally found the key ingredients, Cookworthy spent several years experimenting with just the right balance needed to make true hard-paste porcelain. In 1768, he obtained a patent and opened the Plymouth Porcelain Manufactory. In 1774, Richard Champion bought out Cookworthy and was instrumental in promoting a shift away from the Rococo style that dominated the eighteenth century to the neoclassical style inspired by work in Sevres and Meissen. In 1751, Dr. John Wall and pharmacist William Davis developed a recipe for soft-paste porcelain and set up business as the "Worcester Tonquin Manufactory." King George III visited the factory in 1788, and granted the company a royal warrant, a valuable honor indicating extremely high quality. Thereafter it became known as the "Royal Porcelain Works."

Assembled English blue and white porcelain tea wares including teapot and cover, two tea bowls and saucers, one fluted tea bowl and saucer, slop bowl, and cream jug, c. 1760–65

MATERIALS/DECORATION: Porcelain decorated with the blue and white "Prunis Root" pattern. Scroll design to the top of the spout and handle, and flower spray to the underside of the spout. The cover of the teapot has a white flower finial.

MARK: Various Worcester crescent marks

DIMENSIONS: Teapot is 6" H × 7½" W × 5" diameter

MAKER: First Period Worcester

PROVENANCE: Bonhams, London, at various auctions.

Prunis Root pattern at Worcester

The Prunis Root pattern was used in Worcester over an extended period (1752–1780), and was tremendously popular for regular and miniature sized tea wares. The early pieces were carefully painted with great detail, but as time went on the painting was often poorly executed. To illustrate this we have two miniature teapots: The one on the left was painted around 1760, and the one on the right some ten years or so later. The earlier piece is much more artfully rendered, with fine edges, sharper detail, and an altogether more pleasing presentation.

Miniature tea set probably made for the Dutch market.

English miniature cylindrical tea caddy and assembled miniature tea service, c. 1760–62

MATERIALS/DECORATION: Porcelain with underglaze blue decoration in the "Prunis Root" pattern.

MARK: Various underglaze blue marks

DIMENSIONS: Tea caddy is 2⅜" H × 1⅝" diameter

MAKER: Worcester

PROVENANCE: Tea caddy, cups, and saucers: Simon Spero, London. Sugar bowl and jugs: Peter Hall, London.

NOTES: A similar caddy (with a flat cover) was exhibited in the 2002 Tea, Trade And Tea Cannisters exhibition at Stockspring Antiques, London, appearing in the catalog of that event (number 140). In his book *The Simpson Collection Of Eighteenth Century English Blue And White Miniature Porcelain*, Simon Spero writes:

Miniature cylindrical tea canisters are extremely scarce and only two or three examples are known. The shape was derived directly from a Dutch miniature silver original and one example, in the Zorensky Collection, is complete with its flattened cover. The sugar bowl, different in shape and proportions to the orthodox example, is also derived from Dutch miniature silver. Neither form has a counterpart in full size Worcester porcelain.

English ovoid form tea caddy with a sugar bowl, cup, and saucer, c. 1770

MATERIALS/DECORATION: Porcelain decorated in the "Best Queens" pattern with Kakiemon style floral decoration on alternating panels of dark blue and white. Gilt trim.

MARK: Underglaze blue square seal mark

DIMENSIONS: Tea caddy is 5¾" H × 2¾" diameter

MAKER: Worcester

PROVENANCE: The tea caddy was purchased in London; the sugar bowl was purchased in South Bend, Indiana, while touring with the cast of *42nd Street*. On the bottom of the sugar bowl there is a Sotheby's, New York, label and another label reading, "The collection of J. D. & Louise Trabue."

English ovoid form tea caddy on a footed base, c. 1770

MATERIALS/DECORATION: Porcelain with underglaze blue chrysanthemum sprays to the front, with scattered floral and foliate with butterfly to the reverse.

MARK: Unmarked

DIMENSIONS: 4" H × 2 ¾" diameter

MAKER: Christians Liverpool

PROVENANCE: Roderick Jellicoe of London at the New York Ceramics & Glass Fair.

NOTES: A similar caddy was exhibited in the 2002 Tea, Trade And Tea Cannisters exhibition at Stockspring Antiques, London, appearing in the catalog of that event (number 72).

Worcester teapot and caddy

A similar caddy was exhibited in the 2002 Tea, Trade And Tea Cannisters exhibition at Stockspring Antiques, London, and appears in the catalog of that event (number 70).

English teapot, and tea caddy with cover, c. 1770

MATERIALS/DECORATION: Porcelain with blue scale ground and shaped rococo gilt panels with Kakiemon-inspired decoration to the front, reverse, and trim.

MARK: Underglaze blue square seal mark on the tea caddy and teapot

DIMENSIONS: Teapot: 5¼" H × 7½" L × 5" diameter; caddy: 6¼" H × 3" diameter

MAKER: Worcester

PROVENANCE: The caddy is from David Pownall Willis, Plainfield, New Jersey. The teapot was purchased in London.

NOTES: The blue scale decoration was applied directly to the surface of the piece before it was glazed. Upon glazing, the "glos firing" permanently fuses the decoration to the surface. What we see today is exactly what it looked like more than 250 years ago. The enamel and gilt decoration were applied over the glaze, and the piece was then glazed and fired a second time. The gilt, which becomes a dull color after the glazing, was then burnished to a bright golden surface. Gilt is vulnerable to wearing away with day-to-day use. During the 1750s, Worcester began to find its own identity, though it continued to seek inspiration from Meissen and Sevres, including the use of underglaze ground colors. In his book *Worcester Porcelain* John Sandon states:

Underglaze blue was difficult to control when used as a solid ground color—Chelsea and Derby had terrible trouble with theirs. Worcester solved the problem by inventing "Blue Scale." The increased use of blue and white printing meant that experienced blue painters had time to paint tiny blue scales as an attractive and well controlled ground color. The "Blue Scale" ground proved a popular background for birds, floral decoration, and gilding.

English ovoid shaped tea caddy and cover on a footed base, c. 1770

MATERIALS/DECORATION: Porcelain decorated with gilt garlands held aloft by gilt ribbons. Additional gilt trim to the base, shoulder, neck, and cover, which has a flower finial. The decoration of this caddy is attributed to James Giles.

MARK: Unmarked

DIMENSIONS: 6½" H × 3" diameter

MAKER: Worcester

PROVENANCE: Mary Wise & Grosvenor Antiques, London

NOTES: In her book *The Art Of Worcester Porcelain* Aileen Dawson writes the gilding was:

prepared from gold mixed with honey to make it workable, it was applied with a brush and required burnishing, or polishing. Once polished, the piece was fired again at a lower temperature . . . pieces decorated in the workshop of James Giles in the 1770s often have tooled gilding, which gives a particularly luxurious appearance.

English rectangular sloped-shoulder tea caddy, c. 1770

MATERIALS/DECORATION: Porcelain with underglaze blue flower bouquets on both sides, one with a butterfly. There are flower sprays at the shoulder and a double blue band at the base of the neck.

MARK: Filled crescent

DIMENSIONS: 3⅞" H × 2½" W × 1¾" D

MAKER: Lowestoft

NOTES: The Lowestoft Porcelain Factory was active 1757–1802, producing copies from silver pieces or from Bow and Worcester. Lowestoft made items that were less expensive than the fine porcelains they copied, including the marks. The factory was later used as a brewery and malt kiln.

English square shaped tea caddy and cover, c. 1775

MATERIALS/DECORATION: Porcelain with underglaze blue floral sprays to the front and back, each with two butterflies. There are floral sprays at the sides, on the shoulder, and on top of the cover. Two thin blue bands outline the shoulder and base of the cover.

MARK: Shaded crescent

DIMENSIONS: 4" H × 4" W × 1¾" D

MAKER: First Period Worcester

PROVENANCE: From the collection of H. C. Van Vliet, Amsterdam.

English ovoid-shaped tea caddy with reeded body resting upon a splayed foot, c. 1775

MATERIALS/DECORATION: Porcelain decorated with four puce botanical groupings alternating with polychrome flowers and leaves on the body. A turquoise ground panel on the shoulder with a Bruhl pattern border in the German style.

MARK: None

DIMENSIONS: 5¼" H × 3" diameter

MAKER: First Period Worcester

PROVENANCE: Purchased in Rugby, England.

English diminutive rectangular sloped-shoulder tea caddy and cover, c. 1775

MATERIALS/DECORATION: Porcelain with printed underglaze blue floral rose bouquet pattern on the front and reverse. To one side a floral spray and butterfly, to the other a floral spray. The top is similarly decorated with a flower head finial.

MARK: Filled crescent

DIMENSIONS: 5" H × 2½" W × 1¾" D

MAKER: Lowestoft

PROVENANCE: Seekers Antiques, Columbus, Ohio.

English ovoid-shaped molded tea caddy and cover on a footed base, c. 1775

MATERIALS/DECORATION: Molded porcelain with bianco-sopra-bianco panel wrapping around the body and cover. Underglaze blue floral and foliate pendant borders to the base, shoulder, and cover. The cover has a flower finial.

MARK: Underglaze blue filled crescent

DIMENSIONS: 6¼" H × 3" diameter

MAKER: First Period Worcester

PROVENANCE: Purchased in Croydon, England.

English ovoid shaped tea caddy, c. 1775

MATERIALS/DECORATION: Molded porcelain with bianco-sopra-bianco panel wrapping around the body. Underglaze blue pendant borders at the base and shoulder with a large gilt bird in a landscape on the front, and large gilt floral spray on the reverse. There is gilt trim at the base, shoulder, and base of the neck.

MARK: Blue crescent

DIMENSIONS: 4⅜" H × 3" diameter

MAKER: First Period Worcester

PROVENANCE: Estate of Charlton M. Theus Jr. at Stair Galleries, Hudson, New York.

English pair of barrel form tea caddies, c. 1780

MATERIALS/DECORATION: Porcelain with printed underglaze blue variation of the "fence and flowers" pattern on the front; on the reverse two birds fly over a landscape.

MARK: "C"

DIMENSIONS: Each 4¾" H × 3¼" diameter

MAKER: Caughley

PROVENANCE: Purchased in London.

English barrel form tea caddy, c. 1780

MATERIALS/DECORATION: Porcelain with printed blue and white decoration in a variation of the "fence pattern."

MARK: Underglaze blue filled crescent

DIMENSIONS: 5¼" H × 3¾" diameter

MAKER: First Period Worcester

PROVENANCE: New York Pier Show.

English barrel form tea caddy and cover, c. 1785

MATERIALS/DECORATION: Porcelain with large and small pink and puce flower sprays; the base, shoulder, and cover with alternating bands are in two tones of pink with dotted circles. Gilt finial and edging around the cover.

MARK: None

DIMENSIONS: 4¾" H × 3¼" diameter

MAKER: Caughley

PROVENANCE: Roderick Jellicoe of London at the New York Ceramic & Glass Fair.

English ovoid-shaped tea caddy with reeded body and cover, c. 1785

MATERIALS/DECORATION: Porcelain decorated with a large floral bouquet to the front and floral sprays to the body. Deep blue and gold bands accented in laurel sprays to the upper shoulder and cover. The domed cover has a raised flower finial. Gilt accents.

MARK: Underglaze blue open crescent

DIMENSIONS: 6½" H × 3½" diameter

MAKER: Flight Worcester

PROVENANCE: Marian Haber, New York.

NOTES: A similar caddy appears in *Worcester Porcelain 1751–1790 The Zorensky Collection* (p 283, fig. 344).

Large English hipped rectangular tea caddy, c. 1780–85

MATERIALS/DECORATION: Porcelain decorated in famille rose enamels with a pink diaper border and flower sprigs. There is an Acanthus border molding above the base.

MARK: Unmarked

DIMENSIONS: 5¼" H × 3" W × 2⅕" D

MAKER: Baddeley-Littler

PROVENANCE: Stockspring Antiques, London. A similar caddy was exhibited in the 2002 Tea, Trade And Tea Cannisters exhibition at Stockspring Antiques, London, appearing in the catalog of that event (number 116).

English barrel-shaped tea caddy and cover, c. 1790

MATERIALS/DECORATION: Porcelain decorated with
 scattered polychrome flowers to the body and the inset
 cover. Gilt band to the edge of the cover, which is topped
 by a flower finial.
MARK: None
DIMENSIONS: 5" H × 3¼" diameter
MAKER: Caughley
PROVENANCE: Purchased from Tea Antiques,
 Portsmouth, England.

English tapered cylindrical tea caddy and cover, c. 1800

MATERIALS/DECORATION: Porcelain with dark blue
 underglaze flowers with gilt accents and leaves. Tongue
 gilt border to the lower body and around the rim, cover,
 and flower finial.
MARK: Unmarked
DIMENSIONS: 5" H × 3¼" diameter
MAKER: Caughley
PROVENANCE: Purchased on porcelainbiz.com,
 Sparta, New Jersey.

English hipped rectangular tea caddy, c. 1850

MATERIALS/DECORATION: Porcelain decorated with
 ribbon and florets, bands of silver lustre, and iron red to
 the upper body, shoulder, and neck.
MARK: Impressed "WEDGWOOD"
DIMENSIONS: 4 H" × 2¾" W × 1¾" D
MAKER: Wedgwood
PROVENANCE: Estate of Charlton M. Theus Jr.
 at Stair Galleries, Hudson, New York.

English barrel-shaped tea caddy and cover, c. 1870

MATERIALS/DECORATION: Porcelain with underglaze blue printed with a chinoiserie scene of pagodas and a river, highlighted with a gilt band to the base, shoulder, top, and finial. Cover is inset.

MARK: Underglaze blue pseudo Chinese mark.

DIMENSIONS: 5" H × 3¼" diameter

MAKER: Possibly Booth

PROVENANCE: Purchased in South Wales while traveling with my parents.

English Jasperware cylindrical tea caddy with sloping shoulder, c. 1900

MATERIALS/DECORATION: Jasperware with sprigged neoclassical decoration, white on dark blue. Continuous panels of Grecian female figures within a landscape. Florets encircle the sloping shoulder.

MARK: "WEDGWOOD, ENGLAND"

DIMENSIONS: 5½" H × 3" diameter

MAKER: Wedgwood

PROVENANCE: Appleby Antiques of Stroud, England, on Portobello Road, London.

NOTES: Jasperware is a type of pottery developed by Josiah Wedgwood in the 1770s. It is noted for its matte and unglazed biscuit finish, and was produced in a number of different colors, the best known being a pale blue that has become known as "Wedgwood Blue." Relief decorations (typically in white, but also in other colors) are characteristic of Wedgwood jasperware. They were produced in molds and applied to the ware as sprigs.

English Jasperware hipped rectangular tea caddy and cover, c. 1900–1920

MATERIALS/DECORATION: Jasperware with applied oval grape vine wreaths with figural busts in neoclassical style within. Sprigged grapevine pendants to the sides, shoulder, and cover.

MARK: "WEDGWOOD, MADE IN ENGLAND"

DIMENSIONS: 6½" H × 4" W × 3" D

MAKER: Wedgwood

Miniature Derby tea set

English miniature tea service, c. 1921–1965

MATERIALS/DECORATION: Porcelain with Imari coloration.

MARK: Derby mark; impressed mark on tray; "Derby" "V" "22" painted "H". Impressed Derby mark on the tea caddy.

DIMENSIONS: caddy: 1½" H × 1" diameter

MAKER: Royal Crown Derby

PROVENANCE: Estate sale at Russum's Antiques, Crumpton, Maryland.

The Eighteen Steps at Worcester
From the 1875 brochure
A Guide Through The Royal Worcester Porcelain Works:

An ordinary piece of ware will pass through, on the average, at least eighteen different hands or processes after the materials arrive on the ground, before it can be sent out in a perfect state, as follows: The miller, the slip maker, the preparer of clay, the baller, the thrower, the carrier, the turner, the handler, the biscuit fireman, the scourer, the dipper, the glost fireman, the sorter, the printer, the painter, the gilder, the enamel fireman, and the burnisher. When the ware is drawn from the enamel kiln it is carefully sorted. That which has to be re-painted or re-gilt is sent to its proper destination, and that which is finished is sent into the Burnishing Room, where it is distributed to a number of women who perform this last operation. The gold is a dull yellow color, but after it has been carefully cleaned and a burnisher of blood stone or agate has been quickly rubbed over it, it assumes the beautiful bright surface of burnished gold.

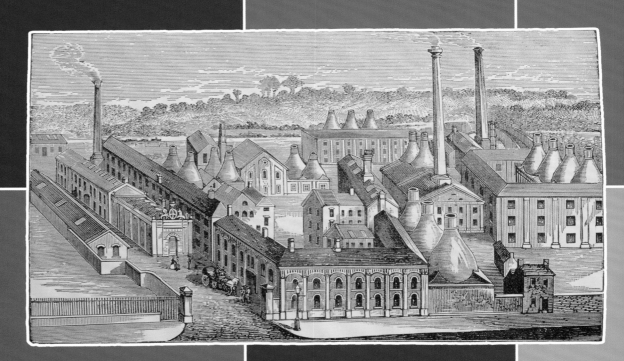

The Worcester factory

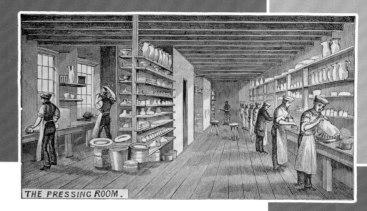

THE THROWER.

THE PRESSING ROOM.

PAINTING ROOM.

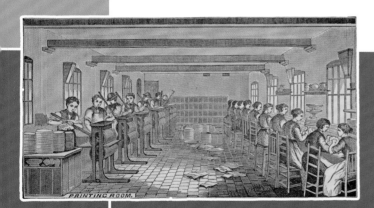

PRINTING ROOM.

BURNISHING ROOM

Chapter 6

CONTINENTAL

In this book, Continental refers to tea caddies made in continental Europe, excluding Germany, which is addressed in a separate chapter. The continental factories include Delft, Sevres, Royal Paris, Royal Copenhagen, Chantilly, Imperial Porcelain Factory, Gardner Manufacture, Samson, The Hague, Royal Vienna, Nyon, and Limoges, among others. The search for the secret ingredients in the porcelain arcanum took hold in France, and Louis XV mobilized his top generals to find kaolin, the key ingredient for "white gold." Around 1768, about the same time the British independently discovered it, kaolin was found at Saint-Yrieix-la-Perche, to the south of Limoges. On February 13, 1771, the Comte de Thy de Milly of the Royal Academy sent the academy a report on the creation of hard-paste porcelain in France. In *The Daily Tea* blog article of September 26, 2014, Anne-Marie Hardie writes:

> Unlike with the British, tea didn't trickle down to the public. The practice of tea drinking in France remained in homes of the elite. And so, tea was seen as a thing of decadence and indulgence. When the divide between the rich and the poor grew in the 17th century, the popularity for a cup of tea vanished. Some authors joke that tea drinking suffered the same fate as Marie Antoinette and King Louis XIV; seen as a drink of the elite, it too met the guillotine.

In their book *The New Tea Companion: A Guide to Teas Throughout the World* Jane Pettigrew and Bruce Richardson write:

> In France in 1648, tea was referred to by a Parisian doctor as "the impertinent novelty of the age"; the playwright Racine drank copious quantities . . . However, despite its favored position in France as the most fashionable drink of the 1680s, tea quickly gave way to coffee, never to regain its early popularity. In Germany, tea was at first drunk as a medicinal brew, but as in France, did not capture the long-term attention of the German people . . . The first tea reached Russia in the early 17th Century when the Mongolian ruler, Altyun-Khan, sent a gift of tea to Tsar Michael Fedorovich . . . At first the drink was consumed only by the Russian elite, but gradually other social groups discovered it and developed their own ways of brewing and serving the infusion. Until the late 18th century, supplies were transported to the Russian market by camels pulling caravans along the "Great Tea Road," which ran from Kashgar, behind China's Great Wall, through the Gobi Desert to Urga, in Mongolia . . . the laborious journey took between 16 and 18 months.

Today, Russia is one of the world's largest consumers of tea, while the people of France, Italy, and Austria are predominately coffee drinkers.

Still Life with Apples in a Delft Blue Bowl by Willem de Zwart. Courtesy of the Rijksmuseum, Amsterdam

Delftware is a blue and white pottery made in and around Delft, in the Netherlands. The manufacture of painted pottery in the Netherlands dates to 1500, when Italian potter Guido da Savino set up shop in Antwerp. While the manufacture of pottery spread throughout the country, the most famous and enduring factories were in Delft, which made various household items, as well as the famous Delft tiles. The seventeenth century is known as the Dutch Golden Age, during which Dutch trade, science, military, and art were among the most esteemed in the world. During this time the Dutch East India Company had a booming business with Asia and imported millions of pieces of Chinese porcelain, which was available to only the wealthiest. In the book *Asia In Amsterdam*, Jaap van der Veen writes: "It was known even in around 1700 that old porcelain, which the Portuguese had imported, was generally of a higher quality than new porcelain." This was because the Dutch East India Company pressed the Chinese to keep prices low. With the death of Wanli Emperor in 1620, exportation of Chinese porcelain disintegrated. In his book *Blue & White: Early Japanese Export Ware*, Martin Lerner notes:

> From around 1620 to 1689, the ceramic history of China is filled with unanswered questions, surprises, and eccentric transitions. What had started out in the beginning of the 17th Century as a reliable source for Europe's insatiable demand for blue and white porcelains . . . by the middle of the century was abandoned. Internal strife, which led to the breakup of the Ming dynasty, brought to an end the trade in export porcelain which the Dutch East India Company had enjoyed with China. The Chinese government's restriction of foreign trade, the interference with shipping by Chinese pirates, and the uncontrolled participation of smugglers of various nationalities in the porcelain market made trade in this once lucrative commodity an untenable business proposition.

It is from this time the Delft potters began to imitate the Chinese originals. By using clay that contained more lime potters at Delft were able to make thinner pieces, and by coating them with tin-oxide glazes followed by a layer of clear glaze they were able to create a good likeness to porcelain. Production spread to England after William III became king in 1689, resulting in many royal commissions. The principal centers for English Delftware production were London, Liverpool, Bristol, and Dublin, Ireland. Today it is difficult to imagine the enormity of the Delft enterprises in the Netherlands. In *The ABC Of English Salt-Glaze Stoneware* J. F. Blacker writes: "the Delft factories, thirty in number, reached their highest prosperity in 1680, when about two thousand persons were employed in them out of a population of 24,000." There are only two Delft tea caddies in this collection.

**Dutch rectangular tea caddy
with replacement silver top, c. 1700**
MATERIALS/DECORATION: Tin-glazed earthenware with
    underglaze chinoserie decoration in Kangxi style featuring
    domestic scenes on the front and back with elaborate vine
    and foliage designs on the sides and top.
MARK: Either a "G" or "6"
DIMENSIONS: 4⅝" H × 3" W × 1¾" D
MAKER: Delft
PROVENANCE: Rob Michiels Auctions, Bruges,
    West-Flanders, Belgium.
NOTES: This piece has a threaded neck for a screw-on top
    and is the oldest caddy in this collection.

Dutch hexagonal tea caddy, c. eighteenth century
MATERIALS/DECORATION: Tin-glazed earthenware
    decorated with blue floral and foliate embellishments
    featuring a large bird to the front with simple scrolls
    to the shoulder.
MARK: Stylized "ARK"
DIMENSIONS: 3½" H × 3¼" diameter
MAKER: Delft
PROVENANCE: Purchased in Chicago.

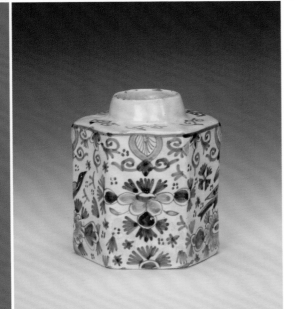

Samson

Samson and Company was a French firm started by Edme Samson in 1845, specializing in reproductions of ceramics for museums and private collections. Chelsea, Meissen, Famille Verte, and Chinese export porcelain are some of the wares he copied. Although Samson claimed his reproductions would be clearly marked as copies, many of his creations have been passed off as originals, leading to speculation he was a forger. The company closed in 1969. Most of the reproduced pieces copy mid-eighteenth to early nineteenth-century designs.

French rectangular tea caddy with canted corners and flat shoulder with French silver mounts, c. 1870–80

MATERIALS/DECORATION: Porcelain with silver mounts. A decoration of garlands of flowers hung from a wide border at the shoulder.

MARK: Indistinct underglaze blue mark; "Mellerio Paris" on the silver mounts

DIMENSIONS: 5¼" H × 4½" W × 3" D

MAKER: Either Samson or Limoges

PROVENANCE: Purchased in Paris while there for the French production of *Barnum* at the Cirque d'Hiver.

A French pair of six-sided ovoid tea caddies and covers in the Meissen style, c. 1870–1900

MATERIALS/DECORATION: Porcelain with each of the six panels decorated with figures in land and harbor scenes. Six-paneled dome covers. Gilt outlines each panel on the body and cover with a gilt finial.

MARK: Underglaze crossed swords and "S" (Samson mark)

DIMENSIONS: 5½" H × 3¼" diameter

MAKER: Samson

PROVENANCE: Pier show, New York.

French rectangular sloped-shoulder tea caddy, c. 1875

MATERIALS/DECORATION: Porcelain decorated in the
Chinese export style featuring a bird in a landscape
standing upon rocks with trees, flowers, and a butterfly
at the front and reverse. Puce diaper border and scattered
flowerets to the shoulder.

MARK: Unmarked

DIMENSIONS: 4¾" H × 3¼" W × 1⅝" D

MAKER: Probably Samson, as the stylized bird and the green
on the famille rose indicates.

A French pair of diminutive vases and covers, c. 1880

MATERIALS/DECORATION: Porcelain decorated with
a Japanese Imari design with flowers and leaves,
and domed covers with lion finials.

MARK: Scratch "H"

DIMENSIONS: 6¼" H × 3" diameter

MAKER: Samson

PROVENANCE: Mimi's Antiques, Columbia, Maryland.

French lozenge-shaped tea caddy and cover, c. 1880

MATERIALS/DECORATION: Porcelain with a coat of arms.
Oak leaf and acorn garland circle the base, shoulder, and
cover. To the front and reverse of the cover draped swag
reads "Nelson 22 April" on one shoulder and "San Josef"
on the opposite shoulder.

MARK: Unmarked

DIMENSIONS: 5" H × 3¾" W × 2½" D

MAKER: Samson

Continental square tea caddy with cap, c. 1880

MATERIALS/DECORATION: The front and reverse are decorated with cockerels and flowering plants, with flower heads on the sides, shoulder, and cover in the Kangxi style.

MARK: Stylized leaf

DIMENSIONS: 3½" H × 3" W × 2½" D

MAKER: Unknown, possibly Samson

PROVENANCE: VenduHuis de Jager, Goes, Holland.

Pair of Large square tea caddies and covers, c. 1880

MATERIALS/DECORATION: Porcelain decorated in the Chinese export style with an armorial panel to the front and famille rose bouquet to the reverse and sides within bianco-sopra-bianco panels. The shoulders and covers are similarly decorated. Gilt trim at the bottoms, shoulders, and covers.

MARK: Unmarked

DIMENSIONS: 5½" H × 4¼" W × 2½" D

MAKER: Samson

PROVENANCE: Gould estate sale at Russum's Antiques, Crumpton, Maryland.

French square tea caddy with canted corners and cap, c. 1880–1900

MATERIALS/DECORATION: Porcelain decorated in the Chinese export style. Bianco-sopra-bianco design frames an armorial coat of arms of a horse and lion with a red and white shield. Famille rose enamel flowers scattered to the body with puce diaper and small flower-filled panels to the shoulder and cover.

MARK: Unmarked

DIMENSIONS: 3½" H × 2¼" W × 2¼" D

MAKER: Samson

PROVENANCE: Gift to mother from Ann Churchill-Brown of Sydney, Australia.

French sloped-shoulder rectangular shaped tea caddy, c. 1880–1900

MATERIALS/DECORATION: Porcelain decorated in the Chinese export style with famille rose enameled flowerets scattered on the body and shoulder. The front features a large armorial coat of arms with a large floral bouquet on the reverse. A deep dark blue band with gilt accents runs along the base, under the shoulder, and to the base of the neck.

MARK: Unmarked

DIMENSIONS: 4⅜" H × 3¾" W × 1¼" D

MAKER: Samson

PROVENANCE: Gould estate sale at Russum's Antiques, Crumpton, Maryland.

French tea caddy and cover in a modified lozenge shape featuring reeded gilt columns to the corners, c. 1880–1900

MATERIALS/DECORATION: Porcelain with enameled birds within a landscape. Flowerets scattered to the green-edged shoulder. Cover in pink and green with gold button finial.

MARK: Gold anchor hanging from a loop

DIMENSIONS: 4⅝" H × 3⅛" W × 2¾" D

MAKER: Samson

PROVENANCE: Stockspring Antiques, London.

Pair of large French rectangular tea caddies with canted corners, sloped shoulders, and covers, c. 1880–1900

MATERIALS/DECORATION: Porcelain decorated in the Chinese style with a large armorial coat of arms on the front and a large floral bouquet on the reverse. A deep dark blue band with gilt accent runs along the base, under the shoulder, and to the base of the neck. Pseudo-Chinese symbol to the shoulders.

MARK: Unmarked

DIMENSIONS: 6⅜" H × 3⅛" W × 2¾" D

MAKER: Samson

PROVENANCE: Gould estate sale at Russum's Antiques, Crumpton, Maryland.

French rectangular tea caddy with canted corners and cover, c. 1880–1900

MATERIALS/DECORATION: Tin-glazed earthenware with front and reverse panels with a landscape scene, canted corners, and a cover with trelliswork. Flowers highlight the trelliswork, shoulders, and cover.

MARK: Unmarked

DIMENSIONS: 5¼" H × 4" W × 2¾" D

MAKER: Samson

PROVENANCE: The Sapphire Gallery, Chicago.

French rectangular sloped-shouldered tea caddy and cover, c. 1880–1900

MATERIALS/DECORATION: Porcelain with a large armorial coat of arms on the front and a large floral bouquet on the reverse. Famille rose enameled flowerets scattered on the body and shoulder. A deep dark blue band with gilt accent runs along the base, under the shoulder, and the base of the neck.

MARK: Faux Chinese mark typical of Samson

DIMENSIONS: 4¾" H × 2½" W × 1½" D

MAKER: Samson

PROVENANCE: Gould estate sale at Russum's Antiques, Crumpton, Maryland.

Large French square tea caddy and cover, c. 1880–1900

MATERIALS/DECORATION: Porcelain with a large pendant tassel and floral swag suspended from a blue ribbon within laurel branches. Laurel leaf garlands to the corners, shoulder, and cover; laurel wreaths and blue bows to the cover. Gilt mounts to the base and cover.

MARK: Faux Sevres mark in underglaze blue

DIMENSIONS: 5½" H × 3¼" W × 3¼" D

MAKER: Samson

PROVENANCE: The Sapphire Gallery, Chicago.

French reeded rectangular sloped-shoulder tea caddy, c. 1890

MATERIALS/DECORATION: Porcelain with a famille rose decoration with small floral spray and insect within a simple roundel to the front and reverse. A small ribbon meander circumvents the piece beneath the shoulder. Simple en grisaille and gilt band along the top of the shoulder.

MARK: Unmarked

DIMENSIONS: 4¾" H × 3½" W × 1½" D

MAKER: Samson

French reeded ovoid tea caddy, c. 1890

MATERIALS/DECORATION: Porcelain with a central panel featuring a coat of arms and crest with scatted floral bouquets and raised white scrollwork on a pale blue body. Gilt trim to the base, base of the neck, and the neck.

MARK: Pseudo Chinese marks to the base

DIMENSIONS: 5¾" H × 3½" diameter

MAKER: Samson

PROVENANCE: Janet K. Fanto Antiques of Easton, Maryland, at the Baltimore Antiques Show.

French rectangular sloped-shoulder tea caddy, c. 1890

MATERIALS/DECORATION: Porcelain with a coat of arms to one side and scattered famille rose flowers to the reverse within a spearhead border. Dark blue bands to the top and bottom with gilt trim.

MARK: "S" and pseudo Chinese marks

DIMENSIONS: 4¼" H × 3" W × 1½" D

MAKER: Samson

French rectangular shape tea caddy, c. 1890–1900
MATERIALS/DECORATION: Porcelain decorated in the
    Kakiemon style.
MARK: Faux hunting horn mark after Chantilly
DIMENSIONS: 5½" H × 3¼" W × 2½" D
MAKER: Samson
PROVENANCE: Stair Galleries, Hudson, New York.

French square tin-glazed tea caddy, c. 1900
MATERIALS/DECORATION: Earthenware with blue
    and white decoration. Front and reverse panels feature
    standing figures beneath trees with birds in the branches;
    side panels have a bird standing upon the ground in front
    of a flowering tree. Scroll decoration to the top of the
    flattened shoulder.
MARK: Stylized letter
DIMENSIONS: 4" H × 2½" W × 2½" D
MAKER: Samson

**French tin-glazed rectangular flat-shouldered tea
caddy and cover, c. late nineteenth century**
MATERIALS/DECORATION: Earthenware decorated in blue
    and white with molded panels to the front and back; one
    of a dandy, the other of a lady holding her dog. This is a
    copy of a Leeds form.
MARK: Underglaze blue "JK" and the number "422"
DIMENSIONS: 5" H × 3¼" W × 2" D
MAKER: Possibly Samson

French lozenge-shaped tea caddy and cover, c. 1900

MATERIALS/DECORATION: Porcelain decorated in the
First Period Worcester style with exotic birds and the
blue ground shoulder with scepter border edged in gilt.
Cover with scattered green florets and a butterfly.

MARK: Faux Chelsea gold anchor

DIMENSIONS: 5⅞" H × 4⅛" W × 3¼" D

MAKER: Samson

French rectangular sloped-shoulder tea caddy, c. 1900

MATERIALS/DECORATION: Porcelain decorated in the
famille verte style. On the front there is a large panel with
a grasshopper upon a flowering plant, and on the reverse
another insect upon a similar flowering plant. Both sides
framed by a green-ground, curl-work border. Yellow and
blue coin design the sides, shoulder, and cover. Later metal
collar to the neck and bottom of the cover.

MARK: Unmarked

DIMENSIONS: 6" H × 3⁵⁄₁₆" W × 1½" D

MAKER: Samson

PROVENANCE: Purchased in Paris.

NOTES: The grasshopper was of special interest, as our family
farm is named for Sir Thomas Gresham and the symbol
for the Gresham name is the grasshopper. The Gresham
family crest is: On a Mount Vert a Grasshopper Or (a
golden grasshopper on a green mound) and it is displayed
by Gresham College, which he founded, and also forms
the weather vane on the Royal Exchange in the City of
London, also founded by him in 1565. Queen Elizabeth I
gave the American land grant to Gresham in gratitude for
his service to the crown.

French tin-glazed, rectangular, flat-shouldered tea caddy and cover, c. 1900

MATERIALS/DECORATION: Earthenware decorated in the Pratt colors of orange, green, and blue with molded panels to the front and back: one of a dandy, the other of a lady holding her dog. This is a copy of a Leeds form.

MARK: "SS" with a line through it, and below that "HO" or "40"

DIMENSIONS: 5" H × 3½" W × 2" D

MAKER: Samson

French rectangular, sloped-shoulder tea caddy, c. 1900

MATERIALS/DECORATION: Tin-glazed earthenware with a central panel framing two blue birds in flight to the front and reverse. Ornate rococo border, body with pink and yellow stripes, and pink vines trailing down the body and sides. There are pink edges at the shoulder, corners, and neck.

MARK: Unmarked

DIMENSIONS: 4⅜" H × 2¾" W × 1½" D

MAKER: Samson

PROVENANCE: Purchased from porcelainbiz.com, Sparta, New Jersey.

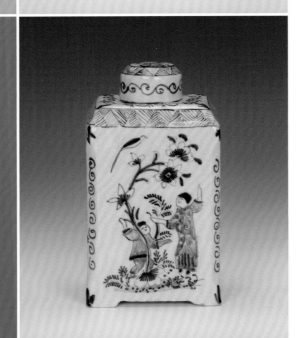

French rectangular tea caddy, c. 1900

MATERIALS/DECORATION: Earthenware with underglaze blue decoration inspired by the Dutch Delft chinoiserie. There are panels with figures within a landscape to the front and reverse, and birds in landscape on the sides. Canted corners, top of shoulder decorated in curl-work, shoulders bordered with triangle-work, and cover similarly decorated.

MARK: Underglaze blue "V"

DIMENSIONS: 5" H × 2¾" W × 2¼" D

MAKER: Probably Samson

PROVENANCE: Zupes Art And Antiques, Hertfordshire, England.

French square tea caddy with canted corners and cover, c. 1900–1910

MATERIALS/DECORATION: Porcelain decorated with large birds and plants in the Chelsea Porcelain style to the front and reverse, with scattered insects to the shoulder. On the top, which might be associated, there is a blue flower.

MARK: Faux Chelsea Porcelain mark of a gold anchor

DIMENSIONS: 5½" H × 3½" W × 3½" D

MAKER: Samson

Other Continental Caddies and Equipage

Austrian rectangular sloped-shoulder tea caddy and cover, together with a cup and saucer and milk jug, c. 1750

MATERIALS/DECORATION: Porcelain with rococo panels in gilt with courting couples: to the front, musicians; to the reverse, an ice skating couple. Scattered flowerets to the body, shoulder, and cover. Feathered gilt scroll to the shoulder and cover. The cover has green leaves and a flower finial.

MARK: Underglaze blue beehive; scratched "S" and painted red "10" underlined, or an "io"

DIMENSIONS: Tea caddy: 6½" H × 3⅛" W × 2" D

MAKER: Vienna Porcelain Manufactory

PROVENANCE: Koller West Auctions, Zurich, Switzerland.

NOTES: The Vienna Porcelain Manufactory was founded in 1718, and is Europe's second oldest porcelain factory after Meissen. The company went out of business in 1864.

Continental rectangular sloped-shouldered tea caddy, c. 1775

MATERIALS/DECORATION: Porcelain decorated with bouquets of flowers and roses to the front and back with plants on the side panels. Two leaf garlands entwine the shoulder and rim.

MARK: Unmarked

DIMENSIONS: 4¼" H × 3" W × 1½" D

MAKER: Unknown

PROVENANCE: Purchased in Paris.

Dutch rectangular sloped-shoulder tea caddy with later ornate silver mounts and cover, c. 1780

MATERIALS/DECORATION: Porcelain decorated with bouquet to the front and reverse, small sprays to each side, and on the shoulder. Cover topped with a double pomegranate finial.

MARK: A stork

DIMENSIONS: 5¼" H × 2¾" W × 2" D

MAKER: The Hague Porcelain Factory

PROVENANCE: Purchased in Copenhagen while there with my parents.

NOTES: Anton Lijncker founded The Hague Porcelain Factory in 1776. He gave the impression that the porcelain was made in his factory, but it is now believed the porcelain was brought in an undecorated state from Germany and Belgium. The factory was short-lived, closing in 1790. Today, pieces from The Hague Porcelain Factory are considered quite rare.

French cylindrical tea caddy (in the Chantilly manner) with ornate silver gilt mounts to the base and cover, c. 1790–1800

MATERIALS: Nyon porcelain with a series of three Chinese figures copying Chinese export mandarin figures decorate the exterior: two standing, one seated on a bench. Ornate silver gilt mounts to the foot and cover with a grape finial.

MARK: Underglaze blue fish

DIMENSIONS: 4¾" H × 3" diameter

MAKER: Nyon Porcelain

PROVENANCE: Koller West Auctions, Zurich, Switzerland.

Russian cylindrical tea caddy and cover, c. 1790

MATERIALS/DECORATION: Porcelain with a tomato red ground. To the front and reverse a large central medallion outlined in gilt contains a rose, stem, and foliage. The front view shows the rose from above and the reverse shows the rose from below. There is gilt trim to the base and bottom of the cover, which has a flower finial.

MARK: Underglaze blue factory mark, Russian "E" for Ekaterina

DIMENSIONS: 3¾" H × 2" diameter

MAKER: St. Petersburg Imperial Manufactory

PROVENANCE: Stockspring Antiques, London.

NOTES: Winogradov and a painter from Meissen called Hunger founded the St. Petersburg Imperial Factory in 1748. Catherine the Great took an interest in the factory, and from 1763, they used the first letter of her name in underglaze blue as their mark. This continued until her death in 1796. The factory was taken over by the Soviet government after the revolution in 1917, and is now Farforovy Zavod Imeni Lomonosova.

Austrian bombe form tea caddy and cover, c. 1800

MATERIALS/DECORATION: Porcelain with large flower sprays to the front and back and flower heads to either side. The cover is decorated in flowerets with a flower stem finial.

MARK: Underglaze blue beehive

DIMENSIONS: 4½" H × 3½" diameter

MAKER: Vienna Porcelain Manufactory

PROVENANCE: Purchased from porcelainbiz.com, Sparta, New Jersey.

NOTES: This shape follows the earlier rococo silver form.

Russian square form tea caddy with canted corners and cover, c. 1870

MATERIALS/DECORATION: Porcelain with a dark blue ground and painted chinoiserie figures within an Asian-inspired cartouche with flower bouquets to the side panels. Flower meanders to the canted corners, shoulder, and neck. The shiny cover suggests it might be a replacement.

MARK: Imprinted "8" and the Gardner mark

DIMENSIONS: 5½" H × 2½" W × 2½" D

MAKER: The Gardner Factory

PROVENANCE: Purchased in Moscow while rehearsing *42nd Street*.

NOTES: Russified English merchant Frans Gardner founded the porcelain factory near Moscow in 1766. The factory produced porcelain, faience, and articles of colored biscuit. Mostly they were tea and dinner services, decorative dishes, trays, vases, and statuettes. The Gardner factory served as important competition for the Imperial Porcelain Factory, inspiring artists at both institutions to produce more complicated wares in terms of form and decoration. The Gardner family operated the factory for three generations until 1891, when it was taken over by Kusnetzoff.

Austrian rectangular tea caddy and cover, c. 1880

MATERIALS/DECORATION: Porcelain extensively decorated with gilt panels with variously colored ground. Gilt meander band to the neck, gilt triangle band, and pink ground with gilt florets to the dome cover. Gilt finial.

MARK: Underglaze blue beehive mark

DIMENSIONS: 4¾" H × 2¾" W × 1⅞" D

MAKER: In the style of the Royal Vienna Porcelain Manufactory

PROVENANCE: New York Pier Show.

French octagonal-shaped tea caddy and cover, c. 1880

MATERIALS/DECORATION: Porcelain with scattered sprays of flowers on the body. Large molded basket weave beneath the flat shoulder and gilt trim.

MARK: Underglaze blue crossed swords and an "E" over a "C"

DIMENSIONS: 4½" H × 3¼" W × 2¼" D

MAKER: Likely Choisy-le-Roy Porcelain

Continental rectangular tea caddy and cover, c. 1880

MATERIALS/DECORATION: Porcelain decorated in green monochrome with courting couples to the front below an armorial crest draped in purple with an ermine lining.

MARK: Unmarked

DIMENSIONS: 4⅝" H × 3" W × 1½" D

MAKER: Unknown

Austrian rectangular sloped-shoulder tea caddy, c. 1880

MATERIALS/DECORATION: Porcelain decorated to the front with the monogram "JM" in floral garlands within a floral garland surround, all upon a gilt trellis ground with floral accents and gilt bead to the sides, shoulder, and reverse. A raised gilt border falls beneath the shoulder.

MARK: Underglaze blue beehive

DIMENSIONS: 4" H × 2¾" W × 2" D

MAKER: Vienna Porcelain Manufactory

French hexagonal shaped tea caddy, c. 1880

MATERIALS/DECORATION: Faience with floral pendant
    design elements terminating in flower heads, alternating
    between green and blue upon the white body. There is an
    ochre band at the bottom and shoulder.

MARK: Underglaze blue "WO/41"

DIMENSIONS: 4¾" H × 3" diameter

MAKER: Unknown

**Continental large rectangular tea caddy and cover,
c. 1890–1900**

MATERIALS/DECORATION: Porcelain with a mythological
    neoclassical style painting of lovers on the front. Sides and
    reverse have dark blue ground and ornate flat, and raised
    rococo scroll panels accented with small white beads.

MARK: Underglaze blue beehive. Front panel signed "P. Heem"
    at the lower right corner.

DIMENSIONS: 5¾" H × 3⅝" W × 2" D

MAKER: In the style of the Royal Vienna Porcelain
    Manufactory

French, child's toy tea set, dated 1891

MATERIALS/DECORATION: The front of the original box
  folds open to reveal a set of four pink and white-checked
  napkins and a round toy cheese or cake, four teacups with
  saucers, four spoons, a pair of tongs, a sugar bowl with
  cover, teapot with cover, and a cream jug, all decorated
  with birds and flower heads.

MARK: Paper label on cover reads "G M PARIS"

DIMENSIONS: Various

MAKER: G. M. Paris

PROVENANCE: Purchased from porcelainbiz.com,
  Sparta, New Jersey.

French rectangular tea caddy with cover, c. 1900

MATERIALS/DECORATION: Porcelain. The front has a lady
   outdoors holding a rose with both hands and smelling it;
   the reverse is two children in colonial dress. Sides,
   shoulder, and cover are mottled olive green.

MARK: The lower right side of the front has the initials
   "M.R.D." and on the bottom "D & C FRANCE"

DIMENSIONS: 5½" H × 3¼" W × 2¼" D

MAKER: Limoges

Austrian rectangular sloped-shoulder tea caddy, c. 1900

MATERIALS/DECORATION: Porcelain decorated with roses
   and florets to the body, shoulder, and cover. The cover is
   related (perhaps from another piece in the service).

MARK: Underglaze blue beehive; green painted crown and
   "SAXE" below the crown

DIMENSIONS: 5" H × 2½" W × 1¾" D

MAKER: In the style of the Royal Vienna Porcelain
   Manufactory

Continental rectangular sloped-shoulder tea caddy with metal and cork stopper, c. 1900

MATERIALS/DECORATION: Porcelain with two named
   panels to each side with an ornate embossed gold panel
   on Mazarine blue ground highlighted with extensive
   gilt decoration. Panels named "Amour and Venus"
   and "Die Erwartung" (the expectation).

MARK: Underglaze beehive

DIMENSIONS: 4¼" H × 2¾" W × 1¾" D

MAKER: In the style of the Royal Vienna Porcelain
   Manufactory

PROVENANCE: New York Pier Show.

Pair of French hipped rectangular tea caddies, one with a cover, c. 1915–30

MATERIALS/DECORATION: Earthenware decorated in the Sevres style with a central continuous panel with flower wreaths and swags between an ornate raised gilded scroll and beaded blue ground to the body and shoulder. Gilt laurel leaves circle the neck. The cover is similarly decorated.

MARK: Enameled crossed arrows without points with a "c" between. One has "Made in France" in red

DIMENSIONS: 5½" H × 3½" W × 2¼" D

MAKER: Unknown

PROVENANCE: Purchased in Paris.

Dutch rectangular tea caddy and cover with bronze fittings, sitting upon ball feet, c. twentieth century

MATERIALS/DECORATION: Porcelain with rust-orange ground and bronze fittings; bands of laurel leaf swags with vases in the neoclassical style. The finial is in the form of a Dutch girl in traditional dress, holding a cup and saucer.

MARK: Unmarked

DIMENSIONS: 5¼" H × 5½" W × 4 ¾" D

MAKER: Unknown

Continental oval-shaped tea caddy and cover, c. twentieth century

MATERIALS/DECORATION: Porcelain with birds to the front and reverse sitting in a tree. There are birds on the cover.

MARK: Written number "2739"

DIMENSIONS: 4¾" H × 3¼" W × 2¾" D

MAKER: Unknown

Pair of continental sloped-shoulder tea caddies and covers, c. twentieth century

MATERIALS/DECORATION: Porcelain with reeded body decorated in overglaze military uniforms in the Chinese export style; fruit and leaf detail to the covers.

MARK: Unmarked

DIMENSIONS: 5⅞" H × 3½" W × 2½" D

MAKER: Unknown

PROVENANCE: Purchased in London.

Dutch rectangular tea caddy with canted corners, c. twentieth century

MATERIALS/DECORATION: Tin-glazed earthenware with underglaze blue flower and scroll design with flowers. Windmill in a landscape on the front and reverse.

MARK: "1288" written over line over stylized four ray fan

DIMENSIONS: 4" H × 3⅝" W × 2¼" D

MAKER: Unknown

Danish sloped-shoulder rectangular tea caddy and cover, c. 1976

MATERIALS/DECORATION: Porcelain decorated with a silhouette of George Washington within a gilt laurel wreath, his signature printed below. Eagle on the reverse; 1776 and 1976 on the sides commemorating the bicentennial.

MARK: Royal Copenhagen around a crown and below that "Denmark". Three wavy blue lines.

DIMENSIONS: 4½" H × 2⅝" W × 1½" D

MAKER: Royal Copenhagen

French rectangular sloped-shoulder tea caddy with rounded corners and cover, c. twentieth century

MATERIALS/DECORATION: Porcelain with ribbon and a floral meander to the upper half of the body and floral sprig to the lower half, front and reverse. Pink and gilt bands to the shoulder and cap cover, gilt finial.

MARK: Paris Royal emblem and under that "Peint a la main"

DIMENSIONS: 6" H × 3½" W × 2½" D

MAKER: Royal Paris

PROVENANCE: Purchased in Rome while there with mother.

Portuguese rectangular tea caddy with rounded shoulder and cover, c. 2000

MATERIALS/DECORATION: Porcelain with decoration featuring a ship under sail, garlands of flowers beneath the shoulder, and a scale work border to the shoulder. Scattered flowerets to the side, shoulder, and cover.

MARK: Printed "INSTITURO PORTUGUES/DE MUSEUS"; made in Portugal by "NG"

DIMENSIONS: 5½" H × 3¼" W × 1⅜" D

MAKER: NG

Chapter 7
WOOD

Chests

Wooden tea chests began to appear in the late seventeenth to early eighteenth centuries. Generally, these were locked boxes with individual glass or silver containers for tea and sometimes sugar. The materials used and designs of these caddies reflect the fashions of the time and they were made by the best cabinetmakers, sometimes with elaborate inlaid decoration. In his book *Tea Caddies Of the 18th and Early 19th Centuries*, Noel Riley writes:

> The earliest wooden tea chests date from the reign of Queen Anne (1665–1714) and most are walnut, but few survive from before the mid-eighteenth century . . . Chippendale published "Six Designs Of Tea Caddies" in the *Gentleman & Cabinet-Maker's Director* (third edition), 1762: they are all in the fashionable rococo style and were probably taken as models by many tea chest makers during the next decade or so. At this time mahogany was most often used, and carved decoration on the corners and feet might be enhanced with elaborate brass or silver handles and escutcheons . . .

Never was there more diversity of shape, material, or decoration than on the tea caddies of the last quarter of the eighteenth century and the first decade of the nineteenth. This makes perfect sense, as The Commutation Act of 1784 had reduced duties on tea from 119 to 12.5 percent, making tea more widely available.

American, Baltimore tea chest, c. 1800
MATERIALS/DECORATION: Mahogany veneers with inlays.
MARK: Unmarked
DIMENSIONS: 7¼" H × 10¼" W × 5¾" D
MAKER: Unknown
NOTES: This is an example of the best Baltimore Federal furniture. Enriched with flame-grained inlays and light wood stringing, and raised aloft on elegant splayed French feet. This chest is replete with characteristics of the most sophisticated Baltimore furniture, despite its diminutive size.
PROVENANCE: This caddy belongs to the collection of Stiles Tuttle Colwill, Baltimore, Maryland.

Wooden Caddies in This Collection

English inlaid tea box with hinged cover, c. 1840

MATERIALS/DECORATION: Wood with an inlaid moth on
 the top, with metal escutcheon with two compartments
 with removable covers, both with metal handles.

MARK: Unmarked

DIMENSIONS: 8" W × 4" D × 3⅞" H

MAKER: Unknown

PROVENANCE: Purchased in London.

English octagonal single compartment tea caddy with hinged cover with elegant outline, c. 1810

MATERIALS/DECORATION: Satinwood with a metal hinge and lock with an ebony escutcheon. There are traces of a silver lining.

MARK: Unmarked

DIMENSIONS: 4½" H × 4½" W × 3¾" D

MAKER: Unknown

PROVENANCE: Purchased in London.

English wooden casket form tea caddy sitting on metal ball feet with hinged cover, c. 1790

MATERIALS/DECORATION: Wood with ivory escutcheon. One internal compartment with a hinged cover for tea and the original glass sugar bowl. Doorknocker handles at each side.

MARK: Unmarked

DIMENSIONS: 6¼" H × 8" W × 4¾" D

MAKER: Unknown

PROVENANCE: J. R.'s Antiques, Queenstown, Maryland.

Large English tea chest sitting on ball feet, c. 1810–20

MATERIALS/DECORATION: Wood with metal hinge and ivory escutcheon and working key. Inside, two compartments with hinged covers and a glass bowl for sugar. Red leather lines the inside of the cover; burlap fabric on the bottom.

MARK: Unmarked

DIMENSIONS: 6" H × 12¼" W × 6" D

MAKER: Unknown

PROVENANCE: Firehouse Antiques, Galena, Maryland.

English square single compartment tea caddy with hinged cover, c. 1860

MATERIALS/DECORATION: Satinwood and ebony banded cube with a metal hinge and ivory escutcheon with key. The caddy sits on four feet.

MARK: Unreadable scratches on the underside of the lid

DIMENSIONS: 4⅜" H × 4⅜" W × 4¾" D

MAKER: Unknown

PROVENANCE: Purchased in London.

English miniature rectangular tea caddy with two compartments, c. 1815

MATERIALS/DECORATION: Mahogany with ivory escutcheon.

MARK: Unmarked

DIMENSIONS: 2⅝" H × 4½" W × 2⅝" D

MAKER: Unknown

English miniature tea caddy with two interior compartments, c. 1825

MATERIALS/DECORATION: Mahogany with square wood escutcheon.

MARK: Unmarked

DIMENSIONS: 2¾" H × 4½" W × 2¾" D

MAKER: Unknown

Chinese square tea caddy and cap cover, c. 1900–20

MATERIALS/DECORATION: Wood painted with a red
    ground with panels in black scrollwork variously depicting
    a figure of a lady in western dress with a bird on her arm,
    birds, a stylized pagoda, and a table set with a jug
    and bowls.

MARK: Unmarked

DIMENSIONS: 5¾" H × 3" W × 3" D

MAKER: Unknown

Japanese tapered cylindrical form, c. 2016

MATERIALS/DECORATION: Wood and lacquer.

MARK: Japanese figure

DIMENSIONS: 4½" H × 3½" diameter

MAKER: Syosen

NOTES: The technique of Yamanaka lacquerware began
    during the late sixteenth century at Lake Yamanaka, Japan,
    near Mount Fuji. The caddy is carved on a lathe with finely
    engraved rings surrounding the body. It is then painted
    with a layer of lacquer. The excess lacquer is wiped off, and
    the caddy is given extended drying time. This process is
    repeated over and over again, and can take up to a year to
    complete. When finished, the caddy is impenetrable and
    protects the tea from air and moisture.

Fruit Form

There was another type of caddy made from the late eighteenth and well into the nineteenth century carved in the shape of a fruit—often in the form of an apple or pear, though melons, pineapples, and peaches also exist. These were made in England and Germany, and were frequently made using the fruit wood appropriate to their shape (for example, a pear caddy made of pear wood); they were inspired by Chinese containers in the shape of an eggplant or aubergine, a good luck fruit. The finest fruit-shaped caddies were made in England and Europe in the late eighteenth and early nineteenth centuries. The interiors were lined with lead foil to protect the tea from moisture, and most have escutcheons, keyholes, and locks made of silver or iron to protect their precious contents. Some were painted as naturalistic fruits, but most are polished or varnished. In *Antique Boxes, Tea Caddies, & Society 1700–1880*, Antigone Clarke and Joseph O'Kelly write:

> I have been unable to find any references for any such caddy being supplied or made. These were turned rather crudely, and it makes me wonder how many were made by grandfather when the family apple tree was felled . . . A few such caddies have survived with a good patina or traces of old color. These have a certain rural charm and, like other "treen" objects, they have mellowed into a comforting folksy tactile familiarity.

These are the tea caddies I most enjoy. I admire the others—the artistry of the Germans, the charm of English creamware, the excess of the Austrians (who really loved their gilt)—but the tea caddies that put a smile on my face every time I hold one are the late-eighteenth-century British fruit caddies. Being wood, they have warmth that silver and porcelain simply do not have.

Pumkin tea caddy courtesy of the collection at Hampton Antiques. Mark Goodger says, "patination and color is everything when it comes to collecting these wonderful treen pieces of art."

Single compartment fruit form tea caddies.

English fruitwood tea caddy in the form of an apple with metal stem and escutcheon, c. 1790

MATERIAL/DECORATION: Fruitwood with tiny sections of red paint still visible, with traces of the lead lining. The bottom has a hole that has been visibly plugged.

MARK: Unmarked

DIMENSIONS: 4" H × 4½" diameter

MAKER: Unknown

PROVENANCE: Walpole's Antiques, Portobello Road, London.

English hinged fruitwood tea caddy in the shape of a pear with metal escutcheon, c. 1790

MATERIALS/DECORATION: Fruitwood with traces of the lead lining. The bottom has a hole that has been visibly plugged.

MARK: Unmarked

DIMENSIONS: 6¾" H × 4¼" diameter

MAKER: Unknown

PROVENANCE: June & Tony Stone Fine Antique Boxes of London, at the Fall Antiques Show, Park Avenue Armory, New York.

Extremely rare English tea caddy in the form of a peach, with original steel escutcheon and stalk, c. 1790

MATERIALS/DECORATION: Fruitwood painted realistically as a peach with a green leaf to one side. There are traces of the original lead lining.

MARK: Unmarked

DIMENSIONS: 5" H × 4½" diameter

MAKER: Unknown

PROVENANCE: June & Tony Stone Fine Antique Boxes, London.

English tea caddy in the form of an apple, c. 1835

MATERIALS/DECORATION: Fruitwood with metal hinge, steel escutcheon, and button finial. There are traces of the original lead lining. The bottom has a hole that has been visibly plugged.

MARK: Unmarked

DIMENSIONS: 4½" H × 4⅝" diameter

MAKER: Unknown

PROVENANCE: Alex Cooper Auctioneers, Towson, Maryland.

Continental fruitwood tea caddy in the form of an apple, c. nineteenth century

MATERIALS/DECORATION: Fruitwood with hinged cover and re-silvered interior. Missing keyhole, which implies a later date.

MARK: Unmarked

DIMENSIONS: 4" H × 4" W × 4" D

MAKER: Unknown

PROVENANCE: Purchased in Paris.

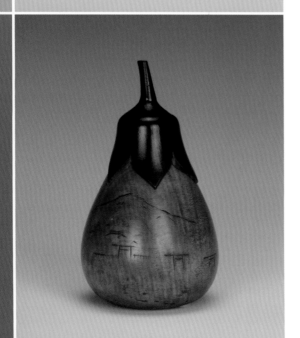

Japanese wooden tea caddy in the form of an eggplant, c. 1860

MATERIALS/DECORATION: Wood with minimalist carving of houses with a mountain peak behind. The cover, a darker colored wood, screws off.

MARK: Unmarked

DIMENSIONS: 5½" H × 3" diameter

MAKER: Unknown

PROVENANCE: June & Tony Stone Fine Antique Boxes, London.

Large Continental fruitwood hinged caddy in the form of a pear, c. 1880

MATERIALS/DECORATION: Wood with metal hinge, escutcheon, and key. Wooden stalk. Silvered foil interior. When the felt on the bottom is lifted, there is no hole and plug. Very dark finish.

MARK: Unmarked

DIMENSIONS: 8" H × 4½" diameter

MAKER: Unknown

PROVENANCE: Purchased on Portobello Road, London.

English fruitwood tea caddy in the shape of an apple, c. nineteenth century

MATERIALS/DECORATION: Fruitwood with metal hinge and escutcheon; wood stem. The piece has been fixed to a lead base, and from the interior it does not appear to have the hole and plug. Interior re-silvered.

MARK: Unmarked

DIMENSIONS: 4¾" H × 4 ¾" diameter

MAKER: Unknown

PROVENANCE: Leslie Hindman Auctioneers, Chicago.

English fruitwood tea caddy in the form of a pear, c. nineteenth century

MATERIALS/DECORATION: Fruitwood with metal hinge, and escutcheon. The bottom has a hole, but the plug is missing. The stem has been replaced.

MARK: Unmarked

DIMENSIONS: 7" H × 5" diameter

MAKER: Unknown

PROVENANCE: New Orleans Auction Galleries.

Possibly French fruitwood tea caddy in the form of a pear, c. nineteenth century

MATERIALS/DECORATION: Fruitwood with metal hinge, but no lock. There is a hole in the bottom that has been visibly plugged.

MARK: Unmarked

DIMENSIONS: 6⅜" H × 4¼" diameter

MAKER: Unknown

PROVENANCE: Purchased in Munich, Germany.

Large English wooden tea caddy in the form of a pineapple, c. 1870

MATERIALS/DECORATION: Wood with carved leaves, with a hinged cover and metal escutcheon and key. The painted finish is very delicate and flaking considerably.

MARK: Unmarked

DIMENSIONS: 8" H × 4" diameter.

MAKER: Unknown

PROVENANCE: Purchased in London.

Continental fruitwood tea caddy in the form of an apple, c. late eighteenth to mid-nineteenth century

MATERIALS/DECORATION: Fruitwood with metal stem, lock, and key. There is a hole in the bottom that has been visibly plugged. The lining is gilded rather than silver and the piece is very shiny and polished, suggesting it might have been refinished.

MARK: Unmarked

DIMENSIONS: 4¾" H × 4¼" diameter

MAKER: Unknown

PROVENANCE: Purchased in Vienna, Austria.

English spalted fruitwood tea caddy in the form of a melon, c. nineteenth to twentieth century

MATERIALS/DECORATION: Spalted fruitwood with metal
    hinge and a wooden stem. The escutcheon is inlaid wood.
    There is no hole or plug in the bottom.
MARK: Unmarked
DIMENSIONS: 5½" H × 4" diameter
MAKER: Unknown
PROVENANCE: Leslie Hindman Auctioneers, Chicago.

English fruitwood tea caddy in the form of a melon, c. twentieth century

MATERIALS/DECORATION: Fruitwood with metal hinge,
    escutcheon, and key with a thick wooden stem. The
    bottom has a hole that has been visibly plugged.
MARK: Unmarked
DIMENSIONS: 5½" H × 4½" diameter
MAKER: Unknown
PROVENANCE: New Orleans Auction Galleries.
NOTES: I purchased this piece from New Orleans Auction
    Galleries, where it was advertised as a "George III, last
    quarter of the eighteenth Century melon tea caddy." When
    Paul Vandekar and Deidre Healy saw it, they told me it
    was a reproduction. I could not believe it, and asked
    Graham Walpole, of Walpole's Antiques in London, for a
    second opinion. This is Graham's response:

I rather agree with your advisors. Probably late twentieth
century. Interestingly, it underlines the pitfalls of relying
on tell tale indicators such as plugs in the base (!). It is
my firm opinion, formed over these past years, that these
caddies are definitely mainland European; German(ish).
In line with this thinking is the fact that the fittings are,
and always should be, steel. If they were English, the
fittings would much more likely be brass, and further
to this will employ a round pin in the upper part (lid)
locating into a round hole in the lock itself. The one on
your melon seems to be rectangular. And again, the hinge
will be of steel and be made to fit the curve of the turned
caddy. I think your hinge may be brass, is nineteenth
century, and is simply recycled from a Victorian box,
probably a low value plain wooden example.

Thomas P. F. Hoving, former director of the Metropolitan
Museum of Art, once wrote in a museum bulletin,
"forgery is not a modern phenomenon. Just after the first
true artist began to do his first work of art, you can be sure
that the first forger began to do his."

The Plug in the Bottom of Fruit Form Caddies

Eighteenth century fruit-form tea caddies have a plug in the bottom where the piece has been attached to a lathe. This is something that the early caddies have that later ones do not, unless they are designed to make something look older than it is. Originals are rare, hard to find, and generally worth a lot of money, making them worthy of counterfeiting. There do not seem to be any known records of a company manufacturing these caddies, adding credence to the theory that they were made at home at pop's workbench, which is perhaps why there are so few of them, and why the originals are so precious. We purchased our first apple form caddy from Walpole's Antiques, from Mr. Graham Walpole on Portobello Road in London. I asked Graham if he would explain the "plug in the bottom," and he explained it thusly:

Bottom of an apple tea caddy showing the hole and plug.

> I have looked into this matter and it is perhaps surprisingly simple. It appears that the chuck (fixing) for the work being turned was, in the eighteenth and nineteenth centuries, similar to this:
>
>
>
> But with the thread steeply tapering, like a threaded cone (see photograph above right). This is from where the plugged hole originates. Modern chucks are variations on these and leave a different mark or no mark like the lower photograph (right).
>
>
>
> As it stands, this evidence suggests that all fakers, or modern day workers, are using a faceplate rather than a traditional screw plate, which would produce a more convincing hole beneath. It is often the case that fakers simply do not understand where they have gone wrong. This may be the case here and trade and collectors alike would wish to keep it that way.

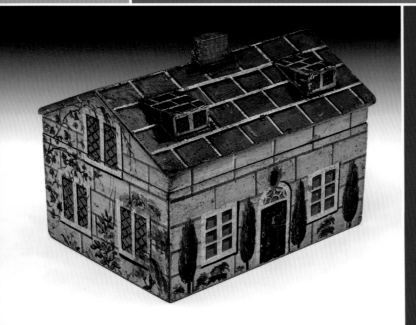

Cottage Forms

Another charming form of wooden tea caddy is the cottage. These are generally from the Regency Period (1811–1820) and have two compartments for the storage of green and black tea. During this period tea caddies became more elaborate, with more complex shapes and footed boxes, some with veneers of tortoise shell, mother-of-pearl, or ivory. The sarcophagus shape, bombe shape, and caddies with carved and inlaid decoration are hallmarks of the Regency Period.

Cottage tea caddy courtesy of Hampton Antiques

English painted tea caddy with hinged cover in the form of a cottage, c. late nineteenth century

MATERIALS/DECORATION: Wood painted as a cottage, sitting upon round metal feet. The piece has been extensively over-painted.

MARK: Unmarked

DIMENSIONS: 6" H × 7" W × 4½" D

MAKER: Unknown

PROVENANCE: Purchased on Portobello Road, London.

Tortoiseshell

Tortoiseshell is produced from the shells of larger tortoises and turtles, and has been used since ancient times for combs, eyeglasses, knitting needles, furniture, musical instruments such as the lyre, guitar picks, and various other decorative objects. The hawksbill sea turtle is a primary source of this material because of its fine color and form. The preparation involves boiling sections of the upper shell (called "scutes") in salt water until they are pliable, then flattening them under a press. Great care must be taken not to compromise the color. Tortoiseshell tea caddies began to appear in the late eighteenth century. These are wooden caddies with a thin layer of tortoiseshell attached to the wooden base, the facets divided by fillets of silver or ivory with silver mounts and handles. Trade in tortoiseshell was banned worldwide in 1973 by the Convention On International Trade Of Endangered Species (CITES). Today stained animal horn, plastics, and other materials have replaced tortoiseshell.

Colored Tortoiseshell Tea Caddies

Mark Goodger of Hampton Antique Boxes and Accessories
explained colored Tortoiseshell tea caddies:

All Tortoiseshell (turtle shell) is applied to a wooden carcass using an animal skin glue; prior to doing this the wooden carcass has to be prepared with a gesso ground, (a hard compound of plaster of Paris or whiting in glue, used in sculpture or as a base for gilding or painting on wood). This is then applied to the wooden carcass and allowed to dry. When completely dry it is sanded, smoothing out any imperfections, allowing for a smoother and nicer finish for the prepared turtle shell to be applied to the carcass. The red, green, and blonde caddies get their color from adding red, green, or yellow pigment to the gesso. These types of caddies have a more translucent shell, allowing this color to be seen clearly.

Tortoiseshell caddies courtesy
of Hampton Antiques

Tortoiseshell Caddies in This Collection

English rectangular wooden box with hinged cover, c. nineteenth century

MATERIALS/DECORATION: Wooden with tortoiseshell veneer and silver seams. Metal escutcheon and sitting upon black bun feet. Inside are two compartments with removable covers featuring mother-of-pearl flower finials. There is a panel on the lid with the initials "MB" and red velvet lining inside the lid.

MARK: Unmarked

DIMENSIONS: 4½" H × 6½" W × 3¾" D

MAKER: Unknown

PROVENANCE: Purchased in Sydney, Australia.

NOTES: We were delighted the initials on the lid were "MB," which happens to be both mother's and my initials.

English wooden pagoda-shaped tea caddy with hinged cover, c. 1820

MATERIALS/DECORATION: Wood with tortoiseshell veneer, silver seams, metal escutcheon, and a metal plaque on the cover with an engraved "W". Woven green paper on the base; traces of silver lining remain.

MARK: Unmarked

DIMENSIONS: 5½" H × 5¾" W × 4" D

MAKER: Unknown

PROVENANCE: Purchased in London.

Ivory tea caddy courtesy of Hampton Antiques

Ivory

Although there are no ivory tea caddies in this collection, they must be mentioned, as they are some of the most beautiful caddies made. Ivory comes from the tusks and teeth of the elephant, walrus, hippopotamus, wart hog, and narwhal (or narwhale), and has been used since ancient times for making decorative items, and even false teeth! Harvesting ivory today is a very controversial subject. The Syrian and North African elephant populations were reduced to extinction, likely due to the demand for ivory. In 2006, nineteen African countries signed the "Accra Declaration," calling for a total ban on ivory trade, and in September 2015, China and the US said they would enact a nearly complete ban on the import and export of ivory. Like tortoiseshell, ivory tea caddies are wooden, with a thin layer of ivory attached to the surface in panels. Mark Goodger of Hampton House Antiques in England shared this photograph of an eighteenth century ivory caddy:

Chapter 8
JAPANNING

Japanning is a form of papier mâché that originated in China during the Han Dynasty (BC 202–AD 220); it was used for making items such as helmets, shields, and furniture. Literally translated, papier mâché means "chewing paper," and it has the great advantage of being strong yet lightweight. Over time, the technique spread along the Silk Road—the ancient trade route linking China to the Mediterranean—into north Persia (modern day Iran), Asia Minor (modern day Turkey), and beyond. By the tenth century, papier mâché was known in Spain, Germany, France, Italy, India, and Japan. In Europe, starting around 1725, gilded papier mâché began to appear as a low-cost alternative to similarly treated plaster or carved wood objects in architecture. Japanese lacquered pieces became popular in England, and in 1740, printer John Baskerville began imitating the highly polished items at his factory in Birmingham. It became known as "japanning." In 1772, Baskerville's associate Henry Clay invented and patented a way to make "new and improved paper-ware" by gluing layer after layer of laminated paper under heat to form tough heat and water resistant panels. His patent describes it: "making, in paper, high varnished panels or roofs for coaches, and all sorts of wheel carriages, and sedan chairs, panels for rooms, doors and cabins of ships, cabinets, bookcases, screens, chimney pieces, tables, tea trays, and waiters." These panels could also be used for smaller objects, such as tea caddies, trays, and boxes. Clay moved to London and set up shop in 1802. On his trade card he described himself as "Japannier in ordinary to his Majesty and to his Royal Highness the Prince Of Wales." In 1816, Clay sold his Birmingham branch to the firm Jennens & Bettridge, but his company in London remained active until 1860.

English George III oval tea caddy, c. 1775–1800
MATERIALS/DECORATION: Papier mâché with metal hinge, doorknocker finial, and escutcheon with lock and key. There is an idyllic country landscape around the body and lid with a fine black line at the shoulder. The interior is lined with lead foil.
MARK: Unmarked
DIMENSIONS: 4½" H × 4¾" W × 2⅞" D
MAKER: Henry Clay
PROVENANCE: Walpole's Antiques, Portobello Road, London. Purchased for a sum, plus two first night tickets to the revival of *42nd Street* at the Theatre Royal, Drury Lane.

English George III oval tea caddy, c. 1780

MATERIALS/DECORATION: Papier mâché with metal hinge, doorknocker finial, and escutcheon with lock and key. There is a rural scene with a herd of cattle to one side and a crowd of villagers picnicking while they watch something in the sky to the reverse. On the lid there are more cattle and a couple riding horseback.

MARK: Unmarked

DIMENSIONS: 5" H × 5" W × 3" D

MAKER: Henry Clay

PROVENANCE: Hampton Antiques, Northampton, England.

English George III square tea caddy, c. 1800

MATERIALS/DECORATION: Black lacquered papier mâché with metal hinge, doorknocker finial, and escutcheon. On the exterior each side has a gilded palm leaf border centering an oval glazed panel with four different neoclassical plaques in the style of Wedgwood jasperware with white figures on a painted blue background. The interior is leather patterned flower and trellis green on black.

MARK: Unmarked

DIMENSIONS: 4" H × 4½" W × 3½" D

MAKER: Attributed to Henry Clay

PROVENANCE: Purchased in Ramsey, Indiana.

Diminutive English tea caddy with hinged lid in the form of a trunk, c. 1851

MATERIALS/DECORATION: Black lacquer with mother-of-pearl inlay. The cover of the inner compartment has mother-of-pearl finial. Metal escutcheon.

MARK: Impressed on the bottom: "JENNENS & BETTRIDGE MAKERS TO THE QUEEN"

DIMENSIONS: 3½" H × 4¼" W × 3¹/₁₆" D

MAKER: Jennens & Bettridge

PROVENANCE: Purchased in Bournemouth, England.

Epilogue

The Mad Hatter's Tea Party. Author's collection

In his book *Tea Caddies Of the 18th and Early 19th Centuries* Noel Riley writes: "Tea caddies of the 18th and early 19th century not only reflect an important and fascinating social custom, but they demonstrate the best craftsmanship in practically every decorative material and technique of the age. It is probably this, together with their endless variety, that makes them so attractive to collectors." My mother was certainly an avid collector. Once in New York I met a dealer at one of the pier shows who had several caddies. As we chatted he told me about an estate auction he had attended on the Eastern Shore of Maryland at Russum's Antiques in Crumpton.

"There were several very nice eighteenth century tea caddies. I bid on them, but always got shut out by a little woman sitting in the front. She bought every single one!"

As he spun the tale I smiled to myself. I knew who that little woman was.

"That was my mother," I told him.

"She's certainly determined!"

Smiling, I said, "I know."

When I ask people if they know what a tea caddy is, I often get the response, "a what?" Most haven't a clue what I'm talking about. It is something that does not exist in the lives of ordinary people in the modern age and we have no reference to it. One colleague thought a caddy was the refreshment trolley pushed through a train car, or in an office during coffee breaks. Another identified it as a quilted cover you put over a teapot to keep it warm, which is actually called a tea cozy. In writing this book, I became increasingly intrigued with the historical eras and conditions that shaped the evolution of the tea caddy. The stories behind the artistic, political, and societal endeavors and experiments to discover the true porcelain arcanum are the stuff of epic motion pictures produced on a grand scale. Most of all, when I view the collection mother and I compiled over several decades, I see tens of thousands of miles of travel, recollect hundreds of memories of places and people, and ponder countless mysteries and histories of who and what are behind each piece. Taken together, this group of caddies tells many tales of times and places that are vastly different from today. Exploring this collection, I have felt like Alice falling down the rabbit hole and happening upon another world—and loving it.

Mother and me.

Acknowledgments

Many people have contributed to this project and I am grateful for their advice and encouragement. In no particular order, they are: Stiles Tuttle Colwill; Peter Warren; A. J. Warren; David Pownall Willis; Leo Kaplan; Alan Kaplan; Margaret Southwell, Stockspring Antiques; Simon Spiro; Michael Linnit; Stair Galleries, Hudson, New York; Graham Walpole, Homewood House Museum; Jonathan Gargulio; Peter Hall; Barbara Hogenson; Gerry Atkins; John Howard; Mary Utterback; James Alley; Rijksmuseum, Amsterdam; Jackson Pearce White at the Victoria & Albert Museum, London; Ralph Russum; Mark Goodger and Matt Lock at Hampton Antiques; Gary Horsey; Dorsey Bramble; Patricia Halfpenny; Patricia Macnaughton; Adam Kidd; David Schmerler; Marshall Troy; Ann Churchill-Brown; Richard Koenigsberg; and Brad Bramble. Special thanks to Paul Vandekar and Deidre Healy, who spent time with me last summer preparing an appraisal of the collection. They enthusiastically unraveled many mysteries, corrected many misidentifications, and exposed a few frauds! Finally, I am grateful to Paul Masse for reading these pages, for his intelligence and sharp editorial eye.

Bibliography

Adams, Brian, and Anthony Thomas. *Chelsea Porcelain.* London: The British Museum Press, 2001.

Adams, Brian, and Anthony Thomas. *A Potwork in Devonshire, the History and Products of the Bovey Tracey Potteries 1750–1836.* Hornsey, UK: Sayce Publishing; 1st edition 1996.

Archer, Michael. *Delftware.* London: Philip Wilson Publishers, 2013.

Arthur, Catherine Rogers, and Cindy Kelly. *Homewood House.* Baltimore: The Johns Hopkins University Press, 2004.

Barker, David. *William Greatbatch, A Staffordshire Potter.* London: Jonathan Horne Publications, 1991.

Barnes, Laurie, Pengbo Ding, Jizian Li, Kuishan Quan, Yoh Kanazawa, and William R. Sargent. *Chinese Ceramics: from the Paleolithic Period through the Qing Dynasty.* New Haven: Yale University Press, 2010.

Branyan, Lawrence, Neal French, and John Sandon. *Worcester Blue & White Porcelain 1751–1790.* London: Barrie & Jenkins, Ltd., 1989.

Buckrell Pos, Tania M. *Tea & Taste: The Visual Language of Tea.* Pennsylvania: Schiffer Publishing, Ltd., 2004.

Chaffars, William. *The New Chaffers Marks and Monograms on Pottery and Porcelain.* London: Reeves and Turner, 1912.

Clarke, Antigone, and Joseph O'Kelly. *Antique Boxes, Tea Caddies & Society 1700–1880.* Pennsylvania: Schiffer Publishing, 2003.

Coenen, Frans. *Glass, China, Silver.* London: T. Werner Laurie, 1907.

Cooper, Emmanuel. *10,000 Years of Pottery.* London: British Museum Press, 2000.

Dawson, Aileen. *The Art of Worcester Porcelain.* New Hampshire: University Press of New England, 2009.

De Sevigne, Marquise de Marie de Rabutin. *The Letters of Madame De Sevigne to Her Daughter and Friends.* Lenox, Massachusetts: HardPress Publishing, 2012.

De Waal, Edmund. *The White Road, A Journey into Obsession.* London: Vintage, 2015.

Dolan, Brian. *Wedgwood: The First Tycoon.* New York: The Penguin Group, 2004.

Doody, Kate, and Brian Taylor. *Ceramic Glazes, The Complete Handbook.* London: Thames & Hudson Ltd., 2014.

Drakard, David. *Printed English Pottery, History and Humour in the Reign of George III 1760–1820.* London: Jonathan Horne Publications, 1992.

Freres, Mariage. *The French Art of Tea*. Paris: Mariage Freres, 2006.

Gallagher, Brian D. *British Ceramics 1675–1825*. London: The Mint Museum in association with D Giles Limited, 2015.

Gibson, Michael. *19th Century Lustreware*. Suffolk: Antique Collector's Club, 1999.

Gibson, Michael, and Geoffrey A. Godden. *Collecting Lustreware*. Great Britain: Barrie & Jenkins Ltd, 1991.

A Guide Through the Royal Porcelain Works, Worcester with Illustrations of the Workrooms; An Epitome of the History of Pottery and Porcelain and the Marks on Worcester Porcelain. Worcester: Deighton & Son, 1875.

Halfpenny, Patricia A., Robert S. Teiteman, and Ronald W. Fuchs II. *Success to America: Creamware for the American Market*. New York: Antique Collector's Club Group, 2010.

Harrison-Hall, Jessica, and Regina Krahl. *Chinese Ceramics, Highlights of the Sir Percival and David Collection*. London: The British Museum Press, 2009.

Hildyard, Robin. *European Ceramics*. London: V & A Publications, 1999.

Holloway, Dr. Chris, and Felicity Marno. *Caughley Porcelain Toy Wares*. England: Monographs on Caughley Porcelain, Vol. 1, 2001.

Kenny, Adele, and Veronica Moriarty. *Staffordshire Figures: History in Earthenware 1740–1900*. Pennsylvania: Schiffer Publishing, Ltd., 2004.

Lawton, Jim. *500 Teapots, Vol. 2*. New York: Lark Crafts, an imprint of Sterling Publishing, 2013.

Lechler, Doris Anderson. *English Toy China*. Marietta, Ohio: Antique Publications, 1989.

Lewis, Griselda. *A Collector's History of English Pottery, 5th Edition*. Suffolk: Antique Collector's Club, 1999.

Lindsay, Irene and Ralph. *ABC Plates and Mugs: Identification and Value Guide*. Kentucky: Collector Books, A Division of Schroeder Publishing Co., Inc., 1998.

Matveyev, Dr. Vladimir. *The Hermitage*. St. Petersburg, Russia: The State Hermitage Museum, 1996.

Mudge, Jean McClure. *Chinese Export Porcelain in North America*. New York: Riverside Book Company, Inc., 1986.

Rickard, Jonathan. *Mocha and Related Dipped Wared, 1770–1939*. New Hampshire: University Press of New England, 2006.

Riley, Noel. *Stones' Pocket Guide to Tea Caddies*. East Sussex: June & Tony Stone Fine Antique Boxes, 2002.

Riley, Noel. *Tea Caddies*. Cincinnati: Seven Hill Books, 1985.

Rontgen, Robert E. *The Book of Meissen*. Second Edition. Pennsylvania: Schiffer Publishing Ltd., 1996.

Sandon, John. *Worcester Porcelain*. Oxford: Shire Publications, Ltd., 2009.

Schiffer, Herbert, Peter and Nancy. *Chinese Export Porcelain, Standard Patterns and Forms 1780–1880*. Pennsylvania: Schiffer Publishing, Ltd., 1975.

Smith, Sheenah. *Lowestoft Porcelain in Norwich Castle Museum, Vol. 2*. Polychrome. Norfolk: Norfolk Museum Service, 1985

Spencer, Christopher. *Early Lowestoft*. Cornwall: Ainsworth and Nelson, 1981.

Spero, Simon. *The Simpson Collection of Eighteenth Century English Blue and White Miniature Porcelain*. Goaters Ltd, Nottingham, 2003

Spero, Simon. *Worcester Porcelain, The Klepser Collection*. London: Lund Humphries Publishers Ltd, 1984.

Spero, Simon, and John Sandon. *Worcester Porcelain: The Zorensky Collection*. New York: Antique Collector's Club Publishing Group, 2007.

Strazdes, Diana, and Sarah Hart Wyckoff. *The Decorative Arts in America at 1776*. Maryland: National Society Daughters of the American Revolution, 1976.

Swift, Jonathan. *Directions to Servants*. London: Hesperus Press Limited, 2004.

Towner, Donald C. *Creamware*. London: Faber and Faber, 1978.

Twinning, Sam. *My Cup of Tea, The Story of the World's Most Popular Beverage*. Hampshire: James & James, 2002.

Twitchett, John. *Derby Porcelain (Antique Collector's Guide)*. New York: Antique Collector's Club Publishing Group, 2002.

van der Veen, Jaap. "East Indies Shops in Amsterdam." In *Asia in Amsterdam: The Culture of Luxury in the Golden Age*, edited by Karina H. Corrigan, Jan van Campen, and Femke Dierks, with Janet C. Blyberg, 134–228. Connecticut: Yale University Press, 2015.

Waller, Edmund. *The Poems of Edmund Waller*. London: Lawrence & Bullen, 1893.

Ware, George W. *German and Austrian Porcelain*. United States: Bonanza Books, 1963.

Wedgwood, Josiah. *The Selected Letters of Josiah Wedgwood*. Edited by Ann Finer and George Savage. London: Macmillan London Limited, 1989.

Wilson, Jane. *Canton China*. Connecticut: Riverside Press, 1966.

Wilson, Timothy, and Luke Syson. *Maiolica: Italian Renaissance Ceramics in The Metropolitan Museum of Art*. New York: Metropolitan Museum of Art, 2016.

Index